The Quest
for Wholeness

Also by Robert Brumet

Finding Yourself in Transition: Using Life's Changes for Spiritual Awakening

Life Transitions: Growing Through Change (audiocassette)

Other "Quest" Books

The Quest: A Journey of Spiritual Rediscovery by Richard and Mary-Alice Jafolla

Adventures on the Quest by Richard and Mary-Alice Jafolla

The Quest for Meaning: Living a Life of Purpose by Jim Rosemergy

The Quest for Prayer: Coming Home to Spirit by Mary-Alice and Richard Jafolla

The Quest for Wholeness

Healing Ourselves, Healing Our World

Robert Brumet

UNITY® Books

Unity Village, Missouri

First Edition 2002

Published by the Unity Movement Advisory Council, a joint committee of the Association of Unity Churches and Unity School of Christianity.

To receive a catalog of all Unity publications (books, cassettes, compact discs, and magazines) or to place an order, call the Customer Service Department: 816-969-2069 or 1-800-669-0282.

Bible quotations are from the Revised Standard Version unless otherwise noted.

Cover design by Jenny Neely

Interior design by Coleridge Design

Library of Congress Control Number: 2001093924

ISBN 0-87159-278-9

Canada BN 13252 9033 RT

Publisher's Note

The books in this series continue the work started by *The Quest* and *Adventures on the Quest* by Mary-Alice and Richard Jafolla. *The Quest* has succeeded in fulfilling its original objectives by effectively presenting an overview of Unity philosophical perspectives and basic beliefs. It also has provided Unity churches and centers a vehicle for individual spiritual growth and has supported community-building by encouraging intergenerational sharing and personal bonding. *The Quest* offers a planned, yearlong exercise in commitment, instruction, and focused learning.

While *The Quest* remains viable in its original form, this new series of books intends a more advanced application of its concept. This series offers a more topic-specific focus and a smaller-book format adaptable to a shorter course of instruction. This series assumes a basic familiarity with *The Quest* teachings.

All the books in this series are endorsed by the Unity Movement Advisory Council, a joint committee of the Association of Unity Churches and Unity School of Christianity.

Acknowledgments

A book is rarely the result of the efforts of one person alone. Such is the case with this book. Many minds have contributed to the final product. I want to acknowledge Michael Maday for his invaluable support, encouragement, and guidance from the beginning to the end of this long project. I wish to thank all members of the Unity Movement Advisory Council for their guidance and review of the manuscript, and in particular, Glenn Mosley, Jim Rosemergy, and Bob Barth for their personal coaching. And finally, I want to thank the many friends and family members who have provided me with support and encouragement throughout this project.

Table of Contents

Introduction

You are about to join me in a quest for wholeness. A quest is a journey—a journey that requires inquiry, investigation, and exploration. Indeed, we will inquire, we will investigate, and we will explore the nature of wholeness. To begin a journey, we need to know where we are starting and where we are going. We need to know how to get from where we are to where we are going. We need to know what to take with us and what to leave behind. And we need to know the dangers, the pitfalls, and what to watch out for in our quest. We will do all these things, and perhaps much more.

Use this book as a guide. It is a handbook for your journey. As a guidebook, it will help you as *you* take the journey. Reading the guidebook is not a substitute for taking the journey. The map is not the territory. The true quest for wholeness is not a book. It is an experience, a very personal experience. Your quest is uniquely yours because you are uniquely you. No one will begin the journey exactly where you are right now. No one else's journey will take him or her to exactly the same places your journey will take you.

Let this be a journey of the heart as well as of the mind. Your heart will take you places where the mind cannot go. Be open to letting your heart lead you. Your mind can tell you *how* to take the journey, but only your heart can tell you *why* you must take it. Only the heart can reveal the deepest mysteries of the quest.

Wholeness is the destination and wholeness is the journey itself. Means and end are one; they cannot be separated. Think not so much about *finding* wholeness; let your quest be one of *becoming* whole as you travel the path. There is nothing to discover but yourself. There is nothing worthy of the journey but the discovery of your Self.

> And the end of all our exploring
> Will be to arrive where we started
> And know the place for the first time.
>   —T. S. Eliot[1]

We begin the journey right where we are and we let it lead us where it will. You will have many traveling companions on this journey. Honor them. Though their paths are not yours, they will help you discover your own path and they will also be your guides along the way. They will do this simply by being themselves and by being in your life. Consider each of them your teacher. Let the journey begin.

---

[1] T. S. Eliot, "Four Quartets," *The Complete Poems and Plays* (New York: Harcourt, Brace, and Company, 1952), p. 145.

Chapter One

Spiritual Healing: The Quest for Wholeness

> To realize healing is to have the awareness
> of God as a living presence, not apart from
> us but the very life in which we live.
>
> —Martha Smock[1]

Spiritual healers can appear in many forms. A spiritual healer may be male or female, young or old, educated or uneducated. He or she may work as a physician, a nurse, a minister, or a counselor. A spiritual healer could also work as a lawyer, an accountant, a carpenter, or a mail carrier. She could be working in any profession. Or she may have no professional title whatsoever. You may recognize her or you may not. You may be one yourself.

A spiritual healer is a person who is dedicated to developing his own wholeness as well as the wholeness of others. He is a person who is committed to his own spiritual awakening and to the awakening of others. A spiritual healer is a person who is willing and able to be a channel for God's healing power—in whatever form is necessary.

Spiritual healing is the process by which we become whole. Yet, in one sense, we are *already* whole, because

3

wholeness is our true nature. Spiritual healing is the process of seeking, discovering, experiencing, and expressing our true nature, which is wholeness itself. Spiritual healing is making visible the wholeness that lies invisible within each of us. To truly understand the nature of spiritual healing, we must first understand our own true nature.

The Foundation of All Spiritual Healing

There is only one Presence, one Power, one Reality. We call that Reality *God*. God is the one and only Reality; there is no other. God is the ground of all being, the foundation of existence itself. We are each an expression of the One Reality. We are each an expression of God. This is our true nature, which is wholeness itself. We are intrinsically spiritual beings, and as spiritual beings, we cannot be sick, poor, or unhappy, because we *are* wholeness itself.

As human beings, we *can* be sick, poor, and unhappy— and many of us are. This is the paradox with which we live: Our potential is great and so is our suffering. Our divinity gets lost in the guise of our humanity.

Humanity is the vehicle through which we are expressing our true nature. We are spiritual beings having human experiences. But most humans believe the converse to be true. Most people believe that they are innately human, and then strive to become "more spiritual." Thus, we have turned reality upside down. Actually, we cannot become more spiritual, because our true nature is Spirit. A Chinese proverb says, "The snow goose need do nothing to make itself white." We need do nothing to become more spiritual.

Human suffering is the result of this reversed understanding of reality. Our experience of suffering is caused by our misplaced identity. Yes, we are human beings but, first and foremost, we are spiritual beings. Spiritual healing is full realization of this Truth.

Once upon a time the young son of a king was kidnapped by a roving band of barbarians. The boy was raised by this tribe and grew to manhood, forgetting about his nobility. Then a famine fell upon the land and most of the tribe died of starvation. As the young man lay alone, weakened by hunger, he had a memory of his childhood. He saw himself as a small child sitting in his father's arms. They sat at a table lavishly covered with every variety of delicious food. This vision gave him the strength to find his way back to the castle. And with every ounce of strength within him, he cried: "Open the door—I am the son of the king. My father awaits me." The astonished guards carried the young man to his father, who once again held his son in his arms.

The Cause of Suffering

Human suffering is the result of believing something to be real that isn't. We have embraced the unreal as real, and as a result, we experience suffering. We embrace facts as reality, and they are not. We embrace appearances as reality, and they are not. Facts change and appearances change. Reality does not.

We each embrace many illusions, for we are educated in unreality from the moment of our birth. The poet William Wordsworth said that "our Birth is but a sleep and a forgetting."² Our "sleep" is not a fault or failing on our part but is simply inherent in our human experience. Our suffering is not a punishment, nor is it a sign that we are sinful or flawed. It is simply a sign that at this stage of our evolution, we are more identified with our humanity than our divinity. This is the present human condition. This is the "sleep" from which we are to awaken.

It is said that soon after his enlightenment, the Buddha passed a man walking on the road. This man was struck by the Buddha's extraordinary radiance and peacefulness of presence. The man stopped and asked:

"My friend, what are you? Are you a celestial
    being or a god?"
"No," said the Buddha.
"Well, then, are you some kind of magician or
    wizard?"
"No."
"Well, my friend, what then are you?"
The Buddha replied, "I am awake."³

The basis of our "sleep" is an alienation from our true nature, which is divine. In this experience of separation from our true nature, we experience separation from others, from the world around us, and from ourselves. We have learned to perceive reality as outside of us rather than within. We have learned to experience ourselves as separate, vulnerable, physical beings surrounded by a potentially hostile world. Our lives are lived trying to protect and defend this vulnerable, separate self.

We are like a man standing on the back of a whale and fishing for minnows. Ralph Waldo Emerson observes that we ignore the "internal ocean" and proceed to go "abroad to beg a cup of water of the urns of men."[4] We are blind to our own greatness, and this blindness is our sickness. To become whole is to recognize our own greatness. We cannot see our greatness as separate beings, but only when we know we are eternally connected to the Source and to one another.

Because of our basic sense of separation, we develop many false beliefs, many illusions about ourselves and others. We may believe that we are unlovable or unworthy or inadequate. We may believe that others are untrustworthy, unlovable, or even dangerous. We may fail to recognize that these beliefs are the product of our personal conditioning and of a culture which tends to perpetuate these beliefs. When we take these illusions to be real, we may experience a great deal of suffering.

Spiritual healing lies in knowing who and what we really are. Intellectual knowing is a start, but it is far from sufficient. Most of our illusions are embedded deep in the subconscious. For healing to occur, the knowing must go as deep as the illusion. Much of the spiritual healing process involves uncovering and healing these illusions buried deep within the mind.

Spiritual healing is replacing error with Truth in our

consciousness. It is becoming free from the limiting illusions that we have unwittingly embraced. "You will know the truth, and the truth will make you free" (Jn. 8:32). Indeed, all healing is a realization of Truth. By this realization we are deeply changed in body, heart, and mind. Spiritual healing is the death of an old and limited way of life and is the resurrection of a new and expanded way of being.

Suffering is the symptom. Believing an illusion to be a reality is the cause of suffering. Realizing the Truth is the remedy. Our primary illusion is a deep-seated perception of separation from our Source, our true nature which we call God. Conversely, the primary Truth, the foundation of all healing, is the realization of our innate oneness with God, our source and our true nature.

Suffering and separation are essentially synonymous. If you have one, then you have the other. They are as two sides of the same coin. Suffering is the tangible side of separation. When the Buddha said that life is suffering,[5] he was referring to life as it is lived under the illusion of separation. He taught the Eightfold Path as a remedy for suffering and separation. When Jesus said, "In the world you have tribulation" (Jn. 16:33), he was referring to the world of separation. When he said, "I have overcome the world" (Jn. 16:33), he meant that he had overcome the illusion of separation. Jesus recognized that "I and the Father [the Source] are one" (Jn. 10:30).

To repeat an earlier statement, our suffering is not

a sign of failure nor is it punishment for our sins. Suffering is part of the human experience because at this point in our collective evolution, we are deeply identified with the experience of separation.

We Are Spiritual Beings

We are spiritual beings having a human experience. Our spiritual nature is the reality of who we are; like the hand in the glove, it animates and gives direction to our human nature. A glove is useful if it fits the hand and if it is flexible and responsive to the movements of the hand. If a glove is stiff and brittle, it is not responsive. If a glove is too large or too small, it does not serve us well. The role of our human nature is to serve as an expression of our spiritual nature. To the degree that it does, we live with ease and joy. To the extent that it does not, we experience suffering and disease.

Unlike the hand and the glove, our human and spiritual natures are not different, in essence. In reality, the body and the mind are spiritual as well. We are spiritual beings expressing ourselves as human beings. We do not wear our humanity as we wear a coat or a hat. The separate categories of Spirit, mind, and body are artificially created simply to aid our understanding. From the mind's viewpoint, they appear very different, yet in reality they are not. By analogy, we see that H_2O can appear in different forms, yet it is always the same substance. H_2O appears in solid form as ice or snow, in liquid form as water, and in gaseous form as vapor or steam. Solid ice appears to be very different from invisible water vapor, yet it is, in essence, the same. The solid body may appear very different from the invisible Spirit, yet it is, in essence, the same.

The distinction between humanness and spirituality is artificial because no real difference exists. The difference is simply one of perspective. We may believe we are *only* human, and that belief creates our human experience. Yet the reality of what we *are* does not change. We use the terms *human* and *spiritual* simply because these are different ways of seeing ourselves. We typically see ourselves as human beings rather than spiritual beings but, in reality, we are simultaneously both.

This recognition that body, mind, and Spirit are of one substance is extremely important in spiritual healing. In the illusion of separation, we not only separate body and mind from Spirit, but we usually separate body and mind from each other. In reality, the body and mind cannot be separated, for they are both, in essence, Spirit.

We create artificial boundaries that may be useful for communication and understanding, but when we think these boundaries are real, we live in a state of illusion. Several times a week I cross the boundary between the state of Missouri and the state of Kansas. As I cross this boundary, I don't feel anything tangible. I could examine the ground with a magnifying glass and I would not see the state line. The state line exists only in the mind of human beings. In a sense, it is a total illusion, and yet it is a very important illusion, for this designation of state boundaries affects the lives of many people. Likewise, the designations *Spirit, mind,* and *body* are important concepts for purposes of our discussion and yet there is no ultimate reality to these boundaries.

Because there is no real division among these various dimensions of our being, there seems to be an interrelationship between and among them. Of course, mind, body, and Spirit affect one another—they are not separate! If you were to jump on one end of a water bed, a person sitting at the other end would be affected. If you were to place a partition between the two of you so that you could not see each other, the other person would still bob up and down when you jumped on your end of the water bed. If this person doesn't know that you are jumping on the other end of the bed, his up and down motions might seem random or capricious, yet there is a very definite cause to the effect that he experiences.

To one who believes that body, mind, and Spirit are unrelated, it may appear that any of these may exhibit random and capricious symptoms. When we see that these dimensions are interrelated, we can see a pattern of cause and effect at work. Our various dimensions of being are related because they are of the same essence.

Conventional medicine and science have largely ignored the existence of our spiritual nature and have historically acknowledged relatively little relationship between mind and body. This has changed somewhat in recent years, but healing professionals are still categorized by the particular level of being—body, mind, Spirit—which they address in their work. Most healing modalities are still confined primarily to the dimension of the symptom. If a symptom is physical, the treatment is usually confined to the physical body—typically in the form of drugs, surgery, or manipulation of the body. If a symptom is mental or emotional, the treatment is generally treated through talk therapy, although it is fairly common for drugs to be prescribed for the treatment of mental and emotional ailments. If a symptom is spiritual, then treatment is usually given by a minister, priest, or rabbi rather than by a physician or psychologist. The spiritual practitioner usually prescribes some form of spiritual treatment such as prayer, penance, forgiveness, or conversion.

Spiritual healing embraces every dimension of our nature. In reality, every level of our being is spiritual; therefore, spiritual healing includes all these levels. In the modern world, we have a clear delineation between doctor, psychologist, and priest, but in the ancient world, this distinction was usually not made. A healer was a healer, and he or she would work with the whole person because mind, body, and Spirit were seen as one.

Spiritual Healing Can Take Many Forms

In our desire for spiritual healing, it is important for us not to be attached to a specific image of how the healing should appear. Spiritual healing manifests itself in as many ways as there are individuals manifesting it. Spiritual healing is a movement toward a greater wholeness of being. This can take many forms.

Spiritual healing can include any form of conventional healing as well as any form of alternative healing. It is not a function of the treatment method but is a function of the view we hold and how we incorporate that view into the healing process. Spiritual healing can occur when we see every need for healing as an opportunity for greater awareness of our true nature and an opportunity to express more of our inherent wholeness.

There are infinite forms of spiritual healing. We typically think of healing as the disappearance of a symptom, but this is not necessarily so. If we have a headache and take an aspirin to make the headache go away, we have not necessarily experienced a healing. The true healing of the headache may require us to explore other physical systems and possibly discover that some system or some organ may be malfunctioning. The healing may require us to review and possibly modify our eating habits. It may require us to change our behavior and the way we live our lives. The healing may require us to examine and possibly modify some of our beliefs and values. It may require us to explore and heal some unresolved emotional issues. It may require us to explore our relationship with God and our deepest sense of identity. Spiritual healing means recognizing the interrelatedness of all aspects of our nature. To be healed is to be made whole. Spiritual healing involves all levels of our being.

It is not uncommon for a spiritual healing to appear miraculous. A so-called miracle is simply an effect produced from an unknown cause. When the cause is known, the healing ceases to be a miracle. It's somewhat like watching a magic show and then discovering how the magician does his tricks. The next time you see the show, you no longer see any "magic," because you now have an explanation. Healings that are common medical practices today would have appeared as miraculous a century ago, because there would have been no explanation for them in terms of the science of that day. There is no limit to what can be healed. There is only a limit to what we can explain.

What we call a *miracle* is miraculous only because of our conditioned and habituated view of the world. Many believe that only Jesus—and perhaps a few other extraordinary people—could work miracles. Yet Jesus himself told his disciples, "He who believes in me will also do the works that I do; and greater works than these will he do . . ." (Jn. 14:12). That which we call miraculous in one era is ordinary in another. At the time of Jesus, what could appear more miraculous than space travel, organ transplants, cloning, and computer networks? Yet today we see these as commonplace.

Conversely, a spiritual healing may not appear as a healing at all in the conventional sense. Sometimes symptoms do not disappear, yet a spiritual healing is taking place. Paul of Tarsus had an enigmatic "thorn . . . in the flesh" which he prayed repeatedly to have removed. The Lord (his own spiritual nature) responded by saying, "My power is made perfect in weakness" (2 Cor. 12:9). The awareness of our spiritual nature may be made more powerful through a weakness of the body or the mind.

It may appear that death signifies a failed healing, but this is not necessarily true. Death itself may be the greatest healing possible when a soul has completed its work in the physical form and is ready to move on. And the process of dying may be a catalyst for deep healing. The awareness of an impending death may provide the motivation to explore aspects of life that may have been ignored during the course of day-to-day living. Relationships may be healed, resentments released, and a degree of surrender achieved that would not be possible when one is embroiled in the mundane facets of life.

Stephen Levine[6] tells of an experience that made him redefine his understanding of healing:

> Robin had been working on healing her cancer, through a variety of techniques, for almost three years. The cancer had gone into remission but after nine months it returned, in force. She was in extreme pain. Robin looked at Levine and asked, "Should I stop trying to heal my cancer and just let myself die?" Deeply moved by the question, his mind had no answer. From his heart he responded, "The real question is, 'Where is healing to be found?'"
> Robin began to investigate the nature of

healing as it related to her condition. At one point she requested a healing circle. Several well-known energy healers formed a circle around her and filled her body with a powerful healing energy.

A week later Robin discovered thirty new tumors on her body. She said, "The healing worked, my heart has never been more open, and it seems the disease is coming to completion." In the three-week period before her death, Robin said that she experienced a sense of wholeness she had never before known.

Healing comes in many forms. Wholeness has many faces. It is essential that we let our minds and hearts become open to healing and wholeness in the very deepest sense of these words.

We are spiritual beings having human experiences. One of the purposes of our human experience is to discover that we are "gods in disguise." Perhaps suffering, in all its myriad forms, is but a symptom of the unawareness of our spiritual nature. We have embraced the illusion of separation from our Source. We have embraced the illusion of "only-humanness." Our suffering is a result of that illusion. We could say that suffering may serve a very useful function. It can serve as an incentive and an opportunity to let go of an illusion and to embrace Truth. It is an opportunity to become more than we have been.

We Are Multidimensional

The experience of spiritual healing always begins with our knowledge of the one and only Reality, the true Source of all life, love, wisdom, and healing. We are expressions of this Source that we call God, the Good. This knowledge is a necessary condition for spiritual healing. If this knowledge is deep enough, it may also be a sufficient condition. That is, it may be all that is necessary. Healing may then occur without any overt change in thinking, feeling, or behavior, and without any physical intervention. Healing may occur from nothing more than a deep realization of Truth.

On the other hand, it may be necessary to change or intervene at one or more of the other levels. Physical treatment of the body may be in order. A modification of diet, behavior, or lifestyle may be necessary. Exploring and releasing suppressed emotions or memories might be called for. A change in one's belief systems, values, or self-image may be required for healing to occur. Spiritual healing may include any or all these factors. Each change is seen to be guided by Spirit and leads to a deeper awareness of Spirit.

An example of a spiritual healing system that includes one or more of the above modalities is the Twelve-Step Recovery program. This program is designed to facilitate spiritual healing for those persons addicted to substances or behaviors that are harmful to them and others. The program begins with an admission that we, functioning solely from our human nature, cannot heal ourselves. Only by surrendering to a Higher Power is healing possible. Some of the steps in this healing process include changing one's behavior, lifestyle, and belief systems as well as asking for and extending forgiveness and making amends, when appropriate. This movement is leaderless, does not follow the teachings of a particular person, and does not proselytize. Yet it is perhaps the most successful spiritual healing movement in the world today. Its success is a testimony to the power of God working through human beings who are committed to spiritual healing.

Ultimately, all healing is a mystery. Whether healing occurs through an apparent miracle or through a conventional medical procedure, the actual mechanism of healing cannot be totally understood. The miracle of life itself can never be totally understood. Just as a farmer can create the conditions for corn to grow but can never make the corn itself grow, so a physician, a psychotherapist, or a spiritual practitioner can create the conditions for healing to occur, but she can never create the healing itself.

Spiritual healing is deep, profound, and mysterious. It is ultimately beyond definition and beyond the understanding of the human mind. But it is not beyond our reach. It is not beyond our ability to experience it. This ability is inherent within each of us. A realization of this Truth was the origin of the Unity movement. Spiritual healing was, and still is, the foundation.

Spiritual Healing and the Origins of Unity

"I am a child of God and therefore I do not inherit sickness."[7] These words echoed in the mind of Myrtle Page Fillmore as she left the lecture given by Dr. E. B. Weeks in the spring of 1886. Myrtle was seriously ill with tuberculosis, a disease she believed that she had inherited and was powerless to overcome. At the time of the lecture Myrtle had been told by her doctors they could do nothing more for her. They said that she had only a limited time to live.

All these somber pronouncements evaporated in the glorious excitement that arose in her soul when she heard she was a child of God and did not inherit sickness. She took this newfound knowledge and put it to work in her prayer life:

> I went to all the life centers in my body and spoke words of Truth to them—words of strength and power. I asked their forgiveness for the foolish, ignorant course that I had pursued in the past, when I had condemned them and called them weak, inefficient, and diseased. I did not become discouraged at their being slow to wake up, but kept right on, both silently and aloud, declaring the words of Truth, until the organs responded. And neither did I forget to tell them that they were free, unlimited Spirit. I told them that they were no longer in bondage to the carnal

mind; that they were not corruptible flesh,
but centers of life and energy omnipresent.[8]

After two years of dedicated spiritual practice, Myrtle
Fillmore was healed. Her body was made whole. Her
heart was filled with the desire to share with others
her spiritual understanding resulting from this healing experience. Friends and neighbors who knew her
marveled at the change that had taken place. Many
were eager to hear how she did it. Before long, many
people were coming to her for help and for guidance.
The results were often astounding.

Myrtle's husband Charles was poignantly aware of
the healing that had taken place in his wife and was
occurring in the lives of many with whom she coun-
seled and prayed. Although Charles was a partial in-
valid stemming from a childhood accident and was in
almost constant pain, he was slow to accept the Truth
that flashed into the mind of his wife two years earlier.
Charles was a businessman, a skeptic. He had difficulty
with the idea of faith in something that seemed so contrary to common sense. Yet the evidence was irrefutable.

He began to study principles of spiritual healing from
a variety of teachers and teachings. Disturbed by what
seemed to be so many conflicting statements and ideas
about a single topic, he decided to take matters into
his own hands. He writes:

> I noticed, however, that all the teachers and
> writers talked a great deal about the omni-
> present, omniscient God, who is Spirit and

accessible to everyone. I said to myself, "In this babel I will go to headquarters. If I am Spirit and this God they talk so much about is Spirit, we can somehow communicate, or the whole thing is a fraud."

I then commenced sitting in the silence every night at a certain hour and tried to get in touch with God. There was no enthusiam about it; no soul desire, but a cold, calculating business method. I was there on time every night and tried in all conceivable ways to realize that my mind was in touch with the Supreme Mind.[9]

At first Charles did not seem to get any results, but as he continued for several months, he noticed that something very interesting began to occur. It would seem that he was being given guidance on business matters in his dreams! As he began to cultivate this awareness, the guidance continued and increased and he had many experiences.

Charles began to apply his spiritual understanding toward his own healing. Results came slowly but surely. After a few years of ardent spiritual practice, his chronic pain ceased, his hip began to heal, and he would eventually dispense with a steel leg extension that he had worn since childhood.

Charles began to throw all his energy into his new-found interest. In April of 1889 he took a giant step: the first issue of *Modern Thought* was published. He declared, "It is not the organ of any school of thought, but the mouthpiece of all honest souls earnestly seeking for spiritual light."[10] This was the beginning of a great publishing ministry that today includes *Daily Word, Unity Magazine,* and many Unity books, booklets, pamphlets, and multimedia products.

One year later the Fillmores took another momentous step. Myrtle announced the opening of the Society of Silent Help. At first this consisted of a small band of friends and neighbors who would sit in silence each evening. They would "meet in silent soul communion every night at 10 o'clock with all those who are in trouble, sickness, or poverty, and who sincerely desire the help of the Good Father."[11]

The following statement was to be held in silent thought for fifteen minutes:

> God is all goodness and everywhere present. He is the loving Father, and I am His child and have all His attributes of life, love, truth, and intelligence. In Him is all health, strength, wisdom, and harmony, and as His child these become mine by a recognition of the truth that *God is all.*[12]

This small group would evolve into what is now the Silent Unity ministry. Silent Unity is more than a group of individuals; it is an activity of Spirit that began more than 100 years ago and continues, in strength, to this day.[13]

Most phone calls and letters to Silent Unity are in response to some experience of human suffering. In one way or another, virtually every prayer request is a request for some form of spiritual healing. Spiritual healing has been and most likely will remain the foundation of Unity's ministry, both at world headquarters at Unity Village and at over one thousand Unity ministries throughout the world.

Mile Markers

- Spiritual healing is the process of experiencing our innate wholeness. Spiritual healers are dedicated to fostering wholeness within themselves as well as others.

- We are spiritual beings having a human experience. Our suffering is the result of having identified exclusively with our humanity, ignoring our spiritual nature.

- The foundation of all spiritual healing is the realization of our innate oneness with God, our true nature, our Source.

- The recognition that body, mind, and Spirit are of one substance is very important in spiritual healing.

- Spiritual healing includes every dimension of our nature.

- There are infinite forms of Spiritual healing. Spiritual healing may appear miraculous or may appear very commonplace.

- Spiritual healing may not appear as a healing at all in the conventional sense. Sometimes symptoms do not disappear, yet a spiritual healing is taking place.

- An experience of spiritual healing was at the origin of the Unity movement.

- Spiritual healing was, and still is, the foundation of the Unity movement.

Chapter One Notes

1. Martha Smock, *Halfway Up the Mountain* (Unity Village, Missouri: Unity Books, 1971), p. 64.
2. William Wordsworth, "Ode on Intimations of Immortality," as quoted in Edward F. Edinger, *Ego and Archetype* (New York: Penguin Books, 1973), p. 10.
3. Joseph Goldstein and Jack Kornfield, *Seeking the Heart of Wisdom* (Boston: Shambhala, 1987), p. 3.
4. Ralph Waldo Emerson, "Self-Reliance," *Essays by Ralph Waldo Emerson* (New York: Harper & Row, 1926), p. 52.
5. The word *suffering* is translated from the Pali word *dukkha*. Another interpretation of this word is *unsatisfying* or *unfulfilling*.
6. Stephen Levine, *Healing Into Life and Death* (New York: Anchor Books, 1987), pp. 1–2.
7. Myrtle Fillmore as quoted in James Dillet Freeman, *The Story of Unity* (Unity Village, Missouri: Unity Books, 1978), p. 45.
8. Ibid., p. 48.
9. Charles Fillmore as quoted in Freeman, p. 52.
10. Ibid., p. 55.
11. Myrtle Fillmore as quoted in Freeman, p. 81.
12. Ibid., p. 82.
13. Unity School of Christianity, Background Information.

Adventure One

Spiritual Healing: The Quest for Wholeness

The real foundation of all effective healing is the understanding that God is Spirit and that man, His offspring, is His image and likeness, hence spiritual.
— Connie Fillmore Bazzy[1]

You are a spiritual being having a human experience. This fact is the basis for your spiritual healing. Yes, you are a human being with a body and thoughts and feelings, but you are also a perfect expression of God. Your human mind may sometimes have trouble fully believing this; nevertheless, it is true.

The work of spiritual healing is to awaken the human mind and heart to this priceless understanding. A need for healing is a need to realize Truth more fully at the deepest levels of our human nature. We do this primarily through regular periods of prayer and by practicing Truth principles in our daily lives. This is the pathway to healing.

---

[1] Connie Fillmore Bazzy, *The Unity Guide to Healing* (Unity Village, Missouri: Unity School of Christianity, 1989), p. 53.

Soul-Talk

I am a child of God. Perfect wholeness is my birthright.

Write this declaration three times, pausing between each line to allow the statement to saturate your consciousness. Then say it aloud or silently as often as possible each day.

1. _____

2. _____

3. _____

Soul-Thoughts

After you have completed writing your Soul-Talk, take time to sit quietly and observe your thoughts and feelings. Write them down.

Note: These questions can be answered privately, through journaling, or they can be the basis for small-group discussions.

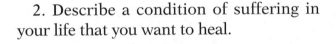

1. Have you ever experienced what you would consider a spiritual healing? If so, describe that healing experience.

2. Describe a condition of suffering in your life that you want to heal.

3. Describe the particular form of suffering that you experience from this condition. Include all levels: physical, emotional, mental, spiritual.

4. How do you feel when you imagine yourself completely free from this condition? Describe this feeling in as much detail as possible.

5. How would you live your life differently if you were completely healed? Be as specific as possible.

Off the Main Trail

 As you close your eyes and consider your condition of suffering, what image forms in your mind? Draw or paint this image.

Stepping-Stone

Read a story about a person who has been healed from the condition you are now experiencing (or one that is similar). Think of this story several times each day.

I am a child of God. Perfect wholeness is my birthright.

Chapter Two

Wholeness: The Destination and the Journey

> The power that created you is always at work to restore you and to maintain you in wholeness.
>
> —Myrtle Fillmore[1]

We have begun the quest for wholeness. A quest is a journey. Most journeys have a destination and our destination is wholeness. But what is wholeness? How do we find it? And is wholeness really a destination or is it to be found within the journey itself?

What Is Wholeness?

Wholeness could mean different things to different people. To someone who is sick or injured, wholeness could refer to the restoration of physical health. To someone anxious, depressed, or mentally upset, wholeness might mean peace of mind, happiness, or joy. If someone is experiencing relationship problems, wholeness could mean love and harmony in relationships. If someone is in poverty, wholeness could mean prosperity. One's particular vision of wholeness may depend upon one's personal need.

We often equate wholeness with physical health. Wholeness might include physical well-being, yet we know that it is much more. Physical health may be the most visible aspect of wholeness, but it certainly isn't the only one. A person could be very healthy physically, but if every other area of his life were dysfunctional, then we would not see him as being in a state of wholeness.

Some may see wholeness as an idealized state of perfection. Most people have a vision of "the perfect life," in which we have no problems and live in a state of perpetual joy and happiness. The particular content of this vision is primarily the result of cultural and familial conditioning. In this picture of wholeness, we may see ourselves as young, healthy, attractive, and energetic, with lots of money to spend and lots of friends to play with. (The picture may be very similar to the life many TV commercials promise if we use their products!) Those with a spiritual orientation may envision wholeness as a state of idealized holiness and perfection. In this condition one is free of all vices, never becomes angry, and lives every moment with a beatific smile on her face. Yet is either of these really the true vision of wholeness? Is wholeness an external condition? Does it need to look a particular way?

Some would say that we are always whole—no matter what our condition or experience. They say that wholeness is our true nature and that we can never be otherwise. Well, this is true at the spiritual dimension of our being, but is it true in every dimension? We may always be spiritually whole, but it's not apparent that we are always physically or mentally whole. Our society and our planet do not appear to be in a state of wholeness.

Wholeness does not have a particular form. We cannot judge wholeness from the outside looking in. We can know wholeness only through personal experience. Wholeness is the natural result of living a Spirit-centered life. It is the natural result of living consciously from the authentic core of our being. In the state of wholeness, we see all things from the perspective of our true nature. Just as all our planets orbit the sun, so everything in our lives revolves around our true identity. This is the state of wholeness.

An all-encompassing definition of *wholeness* eludes us because wholeness itself is a divine idea. We can never totally define a divine idea. It is an idea flowing forth from Divine Mind. A divine idea has infinite possibilities for expression. Wholeness can be expressed in an infinite number of ways.

Another example of a divine idea is love. Love can be expressed in infinite ways. That's why defining *love* is so difficult. *Love* may be impossible to define but we know it when we experience it. The same is true with wholeness. We can fully know wholeness only through our experience of it.

Our hearts may know the true meaning of *wholeness*, but our minds want images and words to describe that inner experience. We will use words to describe various aspects or elements of wholeness, but these words are like different "fingers" pointing to the same basic experience.

So let's look at some words that may be helpful fingers pointing to our destination. We know that no single definition can encompass all aspects of wholeness. Despite the clumsiness of our words, we each know deep in our heart exactly what wholeness is.

These words are both descriptors of the state of wholeness and prerequisites to attaining wholeness itself. Through diligent application, they can lead us to wholeness. They describe both the journey and the destination, both the means and the result of our quest for wholeness.

Self-Awareness

Self-awareness is an essential element in the quest for wholeness. We cannot experience a mature wholeness without it. (An infant or young child may be whole, but that wholeness has not yet matured into a functional wholeness capable of fully expressing itself in the world.) Self-awareness may never be complete because there are infinite facets and infinite depths to our nature. Self-discovery is a never-ending journey.

If we asked the average person if he was self-aware, most likely he would say, "Of course—I know who I am." Most people believe this. When it comes to self-awareness, most of us don't know what we don't know! Paradoxically, the best way to begin the journey of self-awareness is to assume that we know nothing about

ourselves. In this way, our minds are open and unpreju-
diced. In Zen Buddhism this attitude is sometimes
referred to as *beginner's mind*.

We cannot overstate the importance of self-awareness
in the quest for wholeness. So let's explore this topic
of self-awareness. In ordinary awareness, we perceive
everything through a set of filters. These filters are the
result of our conditioning, belief systems, and self-image.
We don't see things as they are; we see things as *we*
are. That's why psychologists can learn much about
someone simply through his or her interpretations of
various inkblots. Our awareness of ourselves is usually
through these same conditioned filters and thus we
keep seeing basically the same thing. This is the reason so many different people can be so absolutely
"right" in their own minds and yet never agree among
themselves. Every day police officers, reporters, judges,
and many others encounter situations in which several people have vastly differing memories of the same
event, yet each is convinced that his particular recol-
lection is the only legitimate view! It is as if everyone
has put on eyeglasses, each shaded a different color,
and then argues over the color of the sky! True self-
awareness is being able to know ourselves beyond the
filters that color our perception of ourselves and everyone else.

Another aspect of ordinary awareness is that our
awareness is usually commingled with our reaction to
what we experience. The mind is constantly judging,
evaluating, and analyzing virtually every experience.

Much of what we call our life experiences are not the result of what we actually experienced, but our minds' *reactions* to what we have experienced. Once again, we see things not as they are, but as *we* are. For example, if I have been conditioned to believe that I am not loved or cared for by others, then I am likely to interpret some actions by others as rejection or lack of caring when that may not be the case at all. If I wave to a friend and she fails to respond, I may experience that as a rejection, when in fact she may not have seen me or may have been preoccupied with her own thoughts. I may feel hurt and use this incident to reinforce my belief that no one loves me. And yet, in reality, my friend may love and care for me very much.

Self-awareness comes from self-observation. Self-observation is closely observing oneself—thoughts, feelings, desires, words, and actions—*without* any judgment, analysis, or attempt to change. We observe ourselves the way a naturalist would observe a bird sitting upon a tree branch—with complete dispassion. The philosopher Jiddu Krishnamurti explains it this way:

> Awareness is observation without condemnation. Awareness brings understanding, because there is no condemnation or identification but silent observation. If I want to understand something, I must observe, I must not criticize, I must not condemn, I must not pursue it as pleasure or avoid it as non-pleasure. There must merely be the

silent observation of a fact. There is no end in view but awareness of everything as it arises.[2]

This is not easy to do, but it is a skill that we can acquire. As with any skill, it develops with practice. Whatever arises in our awareness, we simply pay attention to it without comment. If we find that we *are* judging ourselves, then we simply observe the judgment itself without comment. We pay attention and then we let it go.

"What about change?" you might ask. Paradoxically, change occurs automatically as we observe without judgment. (This is similar to the scientist who knows he will change a quantum event simply by observing it.) The Russian mystic George Ivanovich Gurdjeiff asserts:

> Self-observation brings man to the realization of the necessity for self-change. And in observing himself a man notices that self-observation itself brings about certain changes in his inner processes. He begins to understand that self-observation is an instrument of self-change, a means of awakening. By observing himself he throws, as it were, a ray of light onto his inner processes which have hitherto worked in complete darkness. And under the influence of this light the processes themselves begin to change.[3]

Consciousness itself is a powerful agent of change.

Meditation is also an essential ingredient in the development of self-awareness. Self-observation itself is a form of meditation. Self-observation brings a deeper awareness of our human nature. Meditation brings a deeper awareness of our spiritual nature. With self-awareness we observe the content of the mind. In meditation we experience not only the content but also the context from which all content arises. Both of these practices are vital for the development of self-awareness.

Self-awareness is a prerequisite for wholeness and is also a characteristic of wholeness itself. Self-observation is a powerful tool in the development of self-awareness. This involves moment-by-moment awareness of our thoughts, feelings, desires, words, and behavior. Self-observation means observing everything without judgment—even our judgments. Self-observation and meditation are very powerful tools in the quest for wholeness.

Balance

Another finger pointing us toward wholeness is the word *balance*. Wholeness implies balance. We often think of nature as an example of wholeness. Nature is constantly working toward a state of balance. When free from human tampering, nature is almost always found to be in a state of perfect balance. The science of ecology is teaching us of the complex and delicate balance of nature. Unfortunately, we humans often don't understand this delicate balance of nature until we upset it. Perhaps because we humans, as a species, are not yet whole, we cannot appreciate the quality of wholeness within nature. Maybe if we were truly whole, we would see that we are not outside of nature but are part of it—a vital part of the delicate balance of life on this planet.

Wholeness implies a balance of our physical, mental, emotional, and spiritual natures. We must honor all aspects of ourselves in order to be whole. If we ignore any aspect of our nature, we are out of balance and no longer whole. We may be out of balance and not even know it. Perhaps many in our culture fall into this category.

In our culture most of us overfunction mentally and underfunction physically, emotionally, and spiritually. Our culture favors thinking over feeling and doing over being. This has become our cultural norm. Most of us don't even know that we are out of balance. We have substituted "normal" for natural. (A perfect example of this idea is with the food we eat. Most "normal" food is not natural.) Normal and natural have become two very different things. To live normally in our culture usually means to live in an unnatural way. And sometimes, living naturally requires living outside of the cultural norms.

Perhaps a certain amount of this is inevitable in our fast-paced technological society. Temporarily being out of balance is not necessarily problematic. When we ride a bicycle, we are often off balance, yet we are constantly correcting the imbalance as we ride. But when we accept being out of balance as normal, then we have problems. For many of us, driving cars, wearing high-heeled shoes, and eating fast food are normal activities. They are unnatural but these things need not be problematic if we know that they are not natural and if we take measures to bring our lives and ourselves into balance and thus move toward a state of wholeness. Very often the unawareness of the body and soul doesn't permit us to recognize that we are out of balance.

A healthy body is a body that is in balance. A healthy mind is a mind that is in balance. A healthful lifestyle is one in which body, mind, and Spirit are in balance. Balance in our lives includes balancing time alone and time with others, balancing work and play, balancing rest and activity. A healthful lifestyle means balancing our spiritual practice with our secular life. Too much energy in one area, to the detriment of another, can create an imbalance and a lack of wholeness. A balanced diet of natural foods is wholesome for the body. A balanced life of work and play, solitude and relationship, meditation and activity is a wholesome diet for the soul.

Balance does not necessarily mean equal time or equal measure. Balance means providing necessary time. It means providing time to do what is necessary to bring our lives into balance. The time needed for this will vary from person to person. Eight hours of sleep may be enough for some but not for others. Thirty minutes a day for meditation may be enough for some but not for others. A certain quantity of food may be enough for some but not for others. When we listen to our bodies and our souls we have less need for rules and formulas to tell us what is right for our lives. Referring again to the metaphor of riding a bicycle, we see that no one can give us a formula or set of rules for staying on a bicycle; we must just do it and then moment by moment feel when and where the necessary corrections need to be made.

The question of balance refers not only to our external lives but to our internal lives as well. As a healthy body is in a state of balance, so too is a healthy mind. One way to consider mental balance is to look at the relationship between our thinking and feeling natures. Although it is normal for people to favor one over the other, it is essential that we be able to live effectively with both our thinking and feeling natures. In a state of wholeness, we function with reason and emotion in harmony with each other.

If someone is overfunctioning in his thinking nature and underfunctioning in his feeling nature, then he will not be living life fully. His life may be logical and efficient, but he will never experience the joy of a life lived with passion. When detached from our feeling nature, we are like automatons, analyzing life but never living it. In the novel *Zorba the Greek*, Nikos Kazantzakis describes himself thus: "I had fallen so low that, if I had had to choose between falling in love with a woman and reading a book about love, I should have chosen the book."[4] This man was a prisoner of his own thinking process. By contrast, Zorba epitomized his unlived life. He describes their first meeting: "Zorba was the man I had sought so long in vain. A living heart, a large voracious mouth, a great brute soul, not yet severed from mother earth."[5]

We can, of course, be out of balance in the other direction. A life guided solely by passion is usually a very chaotic life. Such a life may be little more than a soap opera without the commercial breaks. Emotions are wonderful and powerful forces in our lives, but when we let the "wild horse" make our life choices, we are in for a dangerous ride.

The poet Kahlil Gibran likened reason and passion to the rudder and sail of a ship:

> Your reason and your passion are the
>   rudder and the sails of your seafaring
>   soul.
> If either your sails or your rudder be
>   broken, you can but toss and drift, or
>   else be held at a standstill in mid-seas.
> For reason, ruling alone, is a force confining;
>   and passion, unattended, is a flame that
>   burns to its own destruction.
> Therefore let your soul exalt your reason to
>   the height of passion, that it may sing;
> And let it direct your passion with reason,
>   that your passion may live through its
>   own daily resurrection, and like the
>   phoenix rise above its own ashes.[6]

More than fifty years ago the Swiss psychiatrist Dr. Carl Gustav Jung recognized that our modern culture is seriously out of balance. He recognized that we have neglected our instinctual and our intuitive natures. He recognized that our culture is overbalanced with the masculine expression of our nature and underbalanced with the feminine. He observed that most tribal cultures—those that moderns consider primitive— have rituals and myths, stories and dances, traditions and practices that tend to naturally bring them into a sense of balance and harmony with themselves and their environment. Our work, he saw, is not to imitate these cultures, but rather to discover our own stories and the myths and rituals that are meaningful and necessary for the health of our collective soul. He said that we must discover our own stories and bring them forth into expression. The failure to do so is having dire consequences in our society.

And yet, there is cause for hope in today's world. Researcher Paul Ray of American LIVES, Inc., conducted a study of U.S. culture. He found that 26 percent, or 50 million American adults,[7] fall into a group described by him as "Cultural Creatives." These are people interested in values that promote balanced lifestyles such as those relating to spiritual transformation and stewardship of the Earth.

This revolutionary group is described in *Living in Balance:*

> Cultural creatives are called that because they are the innovators giving rise to new ideas and operating on the leading edge of cultural

change. They tend to hold a self-fulfilling optimism regarding the future and are actively involved in building healthier personal, social, and global conditions that are more conducive to harmony and balance. These people tend to be more middle to upper-middle class, and though they are a bit more common on the West Coast, they are found in all regions of the country. Cultural creatives comprise 50 percent more women than men and the overall male-female ratio is 40:60. The commentary on this study holds that in these people lies a great hope for a critical mass of people necessary to make the cultural shift toward a norm of a more balanced and ecologically sustainable way of life.[8]

To be whole is to be in balance. Yet balance is not a static state. It's an ongoing process. Ask any bicycle rider or tightrope walker and you will hear this confirmed. To be in balance is to have a certain equilibrium that tells us when we are out of balance and shows us how to return. This sense of equilibrium is in the soul as well as in the body. If we but listen, both body and soul will tell us what is needed to restore balance.

Integration

Another word that points toward wholeness is *integration*. This word is derived from the Latin *integratus*, which means "to make whole." To be whole is to be integrated, to be in integrity with oneself. The word *integrity*, in turn, means "the quality or state of being complete; unbroken condition; wholeness." This word is derived from the Latin *integritas*, which means "untouched." To be whole is to be integrated, to be in integrity, to have our essential natures untouched, undefiled.

From this lesson in etymology we see that *wholeness* means a state of integrity in which we are at one with ourselves. It means that we are not fractured, fragmented, or internally conflicted. A healthy body is one that is in harmony with itself. A healthy mind is one that is not in conflict with itself. Healthful relationships are not inherently conflicting. A healthy person is one whose body, mind, and Spirit are in harmony.

G. I. Gurdjieff used the metaphor of a horse-drawn carriage to depict the ideal state of integration in humans. His model is that of a carriage, a horse, a driver, and a master inside the carriage. When the system works properly, the master gives instructions to the driver, who in turn directs the horse which pulls the carriage to the master's desired destination. The carriage signifies the human body. The horse signifies the emotions. The driver signifies the mind. And the master signifies the I Am—our divine nature. When we are integrated, the I Am gives direction to the mind, which generates desires and emotions, which in turn motivate the body to take action. Thus the desire of the I Am, the divine will, is fulfilled.

If the system is not integrated, a lack of integrity or lack of wholeness results and the will of the I Am is not fulfilled. If the carriage is broken or the horse is lame, the system goes nowhere. If the horse goes berserk or the driver misunderstands the master's instructions, the system goes in the wrong direction. If our bodies are broken, if we are depressed, it may impair the fulfillment of our divine purpose. If our emotions run our lives or if we don't follow our inner guidance, our lives may move in the wrong direction. Like any metaphor, this one should not be taken too literally, but it does give us a graphic image of the need for harmony among the various aspects of our being.

To be whole is to be integrated, to be in integrity with one's body, mind, and Spirit. To be integrated is to have all aspects of our nature in harmony with one another. To be in integrity is to be authentic, congruent, and genuine. To be in integrity with ourselves is to be in integrity with others and with our environment. When we are out of integrity, we lack wholeness and we may become ill and conflicted with ourselves, others, and our world.

Self-Actualization

Another finger that points in the direction of wholeness is the concept of *self-actualization*. To be whole is to be self-actualized, to be fully functioning as a human/spiritual being. The psychologist Abraham Maslow[9] coined this term. Unlike most psychologists, who directed their attention toward neurotic and mentally ill people, Maslow focused his attention on the mentally healthy. In his research he found a population of individuals who were not just normal and healthy, but super-healthy. These people were as different from normal people as were the mentally ill, only they were at the opposite end of the spectrum.

Maslow saw that these folks are different from most people. They march to the tune of a different drummer. He found that they have very different motivations and values than others. One characteristic he found was that these people tend to live life from the inside out. Most (normal) people adopt the values, goals, and standards that are given them by their culture—values they learn from parents, relatives, teachers, and other authority figures in their lives. The majority of people are motivated primarily by external goals and standards, and their identity and morality are largely determined by outer sources. By contrast, self-actualized people have an internal source for their values, standards, and behavior. Their sense of identity, their morality, their motivations seem to arise from within themselves and often contradict the societal norms. These folks are not necessarily rebels or reformers reacting against external authority, but rather they tend to be somewhat indifferent to outer standards of truth or values and are much more self-referential in making choices. And yet they are not amoral or inconsiderate of others. To the contrary, they seem to possess a stronger sense of morality and deeper compassion than most people. And they are much more stringent than most people in maintaining their personal integrity and commitment to their own values.

Another characteristic of this group of self-actualized people is a high degree of openness to new experiences. Maslow found that most people are open to new experiences only when forced to let go of familiar ways of being. The majority of people will find a certain comfort zone and live within that zone until forced to find new ways. Self-actualized people seem much more willing to leave their comfort zones to experiment with new ideas and activities. They are much more willing to live on the edge of the unknown. Rather than being forced by circumstances to look for new ways, they seem to be natural experimenters who take delight in trying new things.

Most self-actualizers are creative people who enjoy creativity for its own sake. For them the "payoff" seems to be more in the process than in the final product. They are usually more process-oriented than task-oriented and often have little attachment to the tangible results of their efforts. Creativity is not a special activity but simply a way of life. Poet J. Stone describes the self-actualizer's way of living:

> The most invisible creators I know of are those artists whose medium is life itself. The ones who express the inexpressible—without brush, hammer, clay or guitar. They neither paint nor sculpt—their medium is being. Whatever their presence touches has in-

creased life. They see and don't have to draw.
They are the artists of being alive.[10]

Not all self-actualizers are overtly spiritual, yet they all exhibit a strong connection with their inner nature. They usually have a strong sense of what they want and an equally strong sense of what is unacceptable for them. Yet they are typically not willful or aggressive people. They exhibit a high degree of resilience and flexibility and yet often have strong and tenacious desires—usually these desires are for some form of self-expression.

Maslow found that most normal people have strong desires but that most of their desires arise from some perceived deficiency within themselves. Most people have desires for safety and security, for love and belonging, for recognition and approval. These desires are directed primarily toward getting something from someone else in order to fill some perceived inner emptiness. The desires of self-actualizers are oriented more toward self-expression than toward need fulfillment. Instead of being like an empty cup looking to be filled, they are more like an overflowing cup needing to share of itself.

The relationships created by self-actualized people can be characterized in much the same way. They seem much more interested in giving than in taking. This giving is not because of a sense of obligation or codependency but simply because it is their nature to give. Maslow saw that most people love from a sense of deficiency. The object of their love is seen as a fulfillment of something missing within them. On the other hand, self-actualizers love simply because it is a natural part of their being to love. They love out of a desire to share themselves with others rather than from a need to get something from someone else.

Self-actualizers seem to provide much more freedom in their relationships—they can love without obligation or heavy expectations. And yet they can love very deeply. They are not aloof or distant in their relationships but are usually very warm and personable and openhearted, without clinging or manipulating. Maslow went so far as to suggest that this form of love is essential to the well-being of human beings in their developmental years.

To be whole is to be self-actualizing. It is to be moving in the direction of greater self-responsibility, greater self-expression, greater self-awareness, and more unconditional love. To be whole is to become all that we are capable of becoming and to know that the capability itself is constantly expanding.

The Dynamic Nature of Wholeness

Wholeness is dynamic. It is not static. It is not fixed. Wholeness is organic, alive, and evolving. The expression of wholeness at one stage of our lives is not necessarily wholeness at another stage. What is perfectly appropriate for the child may be dysfunctional for the adult (and vice versa). This realization precludes the use of rigid formulas or definitions for wholeness; it may appear to be very different at different times in our lives.

The path to wholeness for one person is not necessarily the path for another. John may need to surrender and trust to move to greater wholeness. Mary may need to apply more effort and will to experience her wholeness. "Different strokes for different folks" is an appropriate slogan.

Wholeness isn't fixed or static. It is open-ended, dynamic, ever-expanding. As we explore these aspects of wholeness, it is important that we not judge others or ourselves. It is equally important not to fall into the trap of comparing ourselves with others or with some idealized condition. Wholeness is an inside job. The only race we are in is the human race, and we will all cross the finish line together!

The Paradox of Wholeness

Wholeness is a paradox. Wholeness is the object of our quest and yet it is our birthright. Spiritually, we can never be other than whole, for we are created in the image-likeness of God, our Father-Mother. Why must we quest for that which we already have? Perhaps we have forgotten our wholeness, and in this forgetting it may have disappeared from our sight. Remembering our wholeness brings it forth into manifestation.

Remembering our wholeness is not like remembering where we put our car keys. It is a far more intricate process. We have buried the memory of our wholeness under many years (and perhaps many lifetimes) of other memories that tell us we are not whole. We have hidden our wholeness in the belief that hiding it is the only way we can survive.

Jack Canfield tells a story that is a wonderful metaphor for how this happens:

> Back in 1957 a group of monks from a monastery had to relocate a clay Buddha from their temple to a new location. The monastery was to be relocated to make room for the development of a highway through Bangkok. When the crane began to lift the giant idol, the weight of it was so tremendous that it began to crack. What's more, rain began to fall. The head monk, who was concerned about damage to the sacred Buddha, decided to lower the statue back to the ground and cover it with a large canvas tarp to protect it from the rain. Later that evening the head monk went to check on the Buddha. He shined his flashlight under the tarp to see if the Buddha was staying dry. As the light reached the crack, he noticed a little gleam shining back and thought it strange. As he took a closer look at this gleam of light, he wondered if there might be something underneath the clay. He went to fetch a chisel and hammer from the monastery and began to chip away the clay. As he knocked off shards of clay, the little gleam grew brighter

and bigger. Many hours of labor went by before the monk stood face to face with the extraordinary solid-gold Buddha.

Historians believe that several hundred years before the head monk's discovery, the Burmese army was about to invade Thailand (then called Siam). The Siamese monks, realizing that their country would soon be attacked, covered their precious golden Buddha with an outer covering of clay to keep their treasure from being looted by the Burmese. Unfortunately, it appears that the Burmese slaughtered all the Siamese monks, and the well-kept secret of the golden Buddha remained intact until that fateful day in 1957.[11]

Like the monks, we hid our "gold" so that it could survive. In a sense, our work is to be like that of the monks, chipping away at the clay covering, curiously searching for the undiscovered treasure within. If we persevere, we will discover the "golden essence" that is our true nature.

Yet this metaphor doesn't tell the whole story. Our wholeness is not a static, inert substance passively awaiting our discovery. It is a living organic essence. The memory of our wholeness often grows and unfolds like a flower. It grows and unfolds because it is a vital, living force constantly seeking to find its way through the many layers of fear and ignorance. And like the flower,

the very soil that buries it also nurtures it. Our wholeness grows from the soil of our own life experiences.

In our quest for wholeness, we may have to do some
digging and chipping to scrape away the false identity
covering our essence. At other times, we must patiently
allow the flower of our wholeness to grow and blos-
som in its own time. The quest is at times an active
process and at times a quiet period of waiting. We need
the courage to chisel, the patience to wait, and the
wisdom to know which to do next.

Mile Markers

- Wholeness is a divine idea. Because we can never totally define a divine idea, wholeness can be expressed in an infinite number of ways.

- Self-awareness is an essential element of wholeness. Self-observation brings a deeper awareness of our human nature. Meditation brings a deeper awareness of our spiritual nature.

- Wholeness implies a balance of our physical, mental, emotional, and spiritual natures.

- Balance refers not only to our external lives but to our internal lives as well.

- To be whole is to be integrated, to be in integrity with oneself. Wholeness implies a state in which we are at one with ourselves—not fractured, fragmented, or internally conflicted.

- To be whole is to be self-actualized, to be fully functioning as a human/spiritual being. Self-actualized people have different values and motivations than most others.

- Self-actualized people live life from the inside out and have a high degree of openness to new experiences. Most self-actualizers are creative people.

- Wholeness is evolutionary, organic. Wholeness at one stage of life is not necessarily wholeness at another stage.

- Wholeness is a paradox. Wholeness is the object of our quest, and yet wholeness is our ever-present birthright.

Chapter Two Notes

1. Myrtle Fillmore, *How to Let God Help You* (Unity Village, Missouri: Unity Books, 1994), p. 117.
2. J. Krishnamurti, *The First and Last Freedom*, as quoted in Vernon Howard, *Mystic Path to Cosmic Power* (West Nyack, New York: Parker Publishing Company, Inc., 1988), p. 119.
3. P. D. Ouspensky, *In Search of the Miraculous* (San Diego: Harcourt Brace Jovanovich, Inc., 1976), pp. 145–6.
4. Nikos Kazantzakis, *Zorba the Greek* (New York: Simon & Schuster, 1952), p. 101.
5. Ibid., p. 13.
6. Kahlil Gibran, *The Prophet* (New York: Alfred A. Knopf, 1945), pp. 57–8.
7. Paul H. Ray and Sherry Ruth Anderson, *The Cultural Creatives* (New York: Harmony Books, 2000), p. 4.
8. Joel Levey and Michelle Levey, *Living in Balance* (Berkeley: Conari Press, 1998), p. 253.
9. For more information about self-actualized individuals, see Abraham H. Maslow, *Toward a Psychology of Being* (New York: Van Nostrand Reinhold Co., 1968).
10. J. Stone as quoted in Levey and Levey, p. 8.
11. Jack Canfield and Mark Victor Hansen, *Chicken Soup for the Soul* (Deerfield Beach, Florida: Health Communications, Inc., 1993), pp. 70–1.

Adventure Two

Wholeness:
The Destination
and the Journey

We are whole creatures in potential,
and the true purpose of desire is to unfold
that wholeness, to become what we can be.
　　　　　　　　　—Eric Butterworth[1]

The quest for wholeness requires understanding the nature of wholeness. Living in wholeness implies living in balance, living creatively, living authentically. Yet all our knowledge of wholeness does little good if we don't engage the quest. Reading the menu will not satisfy our hunger. It is but the first step.

Having a map can aid our journeys yet the map is not the territory. The journey itself is unique for each of us. We must each determine when to work and when to rest, when to be active and when to be quiet. We will discover wholeness but it would be just as true to say that wholeness will discover us. Wholeness is both

---

[1] Eric Butterworth, *Spiritual Economics* (Unity Village: Unity House, 2001), p. 79.

the destination and the journey itself. It is both the seeker and the sought. This is the great mystery of its nature.

Soul-Talk

I am awakening to the realization of my wholeness. I am whole, right now.

Write this declaration three times, pausing between each line to allow the statement to saturate your consciousness. Then say it aloud or silently as often as possible each day.

1. _____

2. _____

3. _____

Soul-Thoughts

After you have completed writing your Soul-Talk, take time to sit quietly and observe your thoughts and feelings. Write them down.

1. Imagine how you would live if you were fully expressing your wholeness right now. Describe this.

2. Looking at your answer to Activity 1, what is the greatest difference you see between the life you described and the life you are living right now?

3. Is your life in balance (a) internally? (b) externally? Record your thoughts.

4. Looking at your answer to Activity 3, what changes would you need to make to bring your life into balance? What are the obstacles to these changes?

5. Name some people who, in your opinion, have exemplified a life of wholeness. Why did you choose these people?

Off the Main Trail

 1. As you think of the state of wholeness, allow an image to come to mind. Describe the image. Draw a picture of it.

2. Have an internal dialogue with that image. Mentally talk to it. Listen to it. Have a conversation with it. Record the results.

Stepping-Stone

 Read a biographical story of one person you selected as exemplifying wholeness. Think of this person several times throughout the week. At the end of the week, notice how this exercise has affected you.

I am awakening to the realization of my wholeness.
I am whole, right now.

Chapter Three

Individuation:
The Pathway to Wholeness

> The experience of Self brings a feeling of
> standing on solid ground inside oneself, on
> a patch of eternity, which even physical
> death cannot touch.
> —Mary-Louise von Franz[1]

Having identified and described our destination, it
would be helpful to have a map showing us how to get
there. In this chapter, we explore a pathway to wholeness mapped by one of the great spiritual pioneers of
the modern era, Dr. Carl Gustav Jung.

Dr. Jung coined a term called "the Self," which he
saw as the archetype of wholeness in the collective unconscious. The collective unconscious is that dimension of mind which is inherited by all human beings.
This level of the unconscious consists not of personal
memories and experiences, but those we have inherited
from the past history of the entire human race. The
collective unconscious consists of instincts and archetypes. Instincts are preexisting patterns of behavior
inherited by every human being. Archetypes are pre-
existing patterns of perception and understanding that
are also inherited by every human being. This means

that the archetype of the Self exists within every human being. It is the essential nature of every human being. The Self is our own spiritual nature; it is the archetype of wholeness. Our life's work is to consciously bring this archetype into awareness and expression in our personal lives. Jungian author Robert Johnson describes it thusly:

> The process can be summed up in one sentence: it is the relocating of the center of the [psyche]^2 from the ego to a center greater than one's self. This superpersonal center has been variously called the Self, the Christ nature, the Buddha nature, superconsciousness, satori, and samadhi.^{3}

Jung called this process *individuation*. It is the process of becoming a true individual. This is the pathway to wholeness.

The Self

Before we discuss individuation, let's explore the archetype of the Self. As an archetype, it is a preexistent pattern within each person. Although it exists as a pattern within each of us, its particularized expression will be different for each person. In one sense there is only one Self, and yet in another sense this Self is unique to each of us. By analogy, let us consider a human organ such as the heart. In one sense, there is only one human heart; we see pictures of it in anatomy books. Yet every human heart is unique, as is every human being.

As Johnson has stated, the Self may generally be equated with the terms *the Christ nature, the Buddha nature,* or *superconsciousness.* The term we will use most is *Individuality,* a word used by Dr. H. Emilie Cady in *Lessons in Truth.* The terms *individuality* and *individuation* are derived from the word *individual,* which has two primary meanings. One meaning is inherent in the etymology of the word—it stems from the Latin word *individuus,* which means "not divisible."

Our human personalities are divisible. Our human personalities consist of many different components. Most of these personality components were developed as survival mechanisms when we were children. As personalities, we consist of many component parts— often unintegrated and sometimes in conflict with one another. The personality is highly divisible and fragmented. By contrast, the Self—the Individuality—is undivided. It is whole, complete, at one with itself. In reality, it is one with all that is. It cannot be divided.

The other meaning of the word *individual* is "uniqueness." *Uniqueness* means that we are each an original edition—there is no duplicate anywhere in the universe! If our personalities alone are considered, our uniqueness is fairly superficial. Functioning solely from the personality, we are relatively predictable. Only in our Individuality are we truly unique. Our Individuality is not simply the product of our personal histories.

It is unconditional. The personality believes that I am this or I am that. The Individuality knows that I *Am*. Only when we discover and express the Self, our Individuality, do we become truly unique individuals. The work of individuation is to discover, experience, and express our Individuality. Thus we experience our wholeness.

Jungian analyst Peter O'Connor writes:

> Wholeness is the goal of the psyche, but this does not occur by chance or some random ordering of the psyche's contents. On the contrary it is organised by the archetype we have termed Self. Hence this Self is often termed . . . the archetype of order, that archetypal pattern, or energy to integrate, to move towards a state of psychological completeness or wholeness.[4]

The Self is both the source and the goal of wholeness; it is both the universal and the individual. It is both our uniqueness and our sameness. It is beyond opposites; it is both the center and the circumference of all that we are. The poet T. S. Eliot called it the "still point":

> At the still point of the turning world.
>   Neither flesh nor fleshless;
> Neither from nor towards; at the still
>   point, there the dance is,
> But neither arrest nor movement.
>   And do not call it fixity,

Where past and future are gathered.
Neither movement from nor towards,
Neither ascent nor decline. Except for
the point, the still point,
There would be no dance, and there is
only the dance.[5]

Individuation

Individuation is the process of achieving wholeness,
of experiencing the Self. In Robert Johnson's words:

Individuation is the lifelong process in which
a person increasingly becomes the whole and
complete person God intended him to be. It
entails the gradual expansion of his or her consciousness and the increasing capacity of the
conscious personality to reflect the total self. . . .
The psychology of individuation . . . shows
that the goal of this process of becoming
whole is not perfection, but completeness. The
whole person is never blameless, guiltless, or
pure but is one in whom all sides of himself have
been combined inexplicably into a total person.
This paradoxical unity of the self, which is like a
combination of opposites, is a secret that cannot
be rationally understood or comprehended.
Unity is, so to speak, a mystery known only to
God. The ego can experience the unity of the self
but never logically comprehend it.[6]

The process of individuation could be described as "the reconciliation of opposites." The "opposites" refer to the opposites within ourselves. The human personality is not a monolithic structure. It is composed of many components or subpersonalities. These subpersonalities are usually paired in polar opposition to one another. We typically identify with only one side of this pair. Normally, we are consciously aware of only one side; the other side is relegated to the subconscious.[7] Passive/aggressive, masculine/feminine, introvert/extrovert, parent/child, victim/victimizer, thinking/feeling—we carry the drama of these (and many other) opposing forces within our consciousness.[8] They show up in our lives in many ways.

These oppositional forces readily appear in our everyday thinking, our inner conversations, and our self-talk. For example, we may have our eyes on a delicious-looking piece of chocolate cake. Desire arises in the mind; an internal debate ensues. After several seconds, the dialogue is over. Let's say that our appetite prevails and we eat the cake. Typically, we no sooner finish our cake than we hear an internal voice saying something such as, "You shouldn't have done that!" We may then find ourselves feeling remorse over our "sin" and then offer the promise of penance: "I'll jog an extra mile tomorrow." (This is a typical inner parent/child dialogue.)

Even a little self-observation reveals a great deal of inner conflict that is virtually continuous. We judge, grade, praise, blame, and ridicule ourselves endlessly.

This voice comes from the conditioned conscience, sometimes referred to as the "superego." It is the internalized voice of parents, teachers, preachers, and other authority figures from our past. The other side of this pair may be the mischievous, rebellious, sometimes repentant child who wants nothing but to have fun and avoid responsibility.

Typically, one side of each conflict resides within the subconscious level of mind. (This is sometimes referred to as the "shadow" side.) We usually identify with one side of the conflicting pair and the other side goes underground—into the shadow land. For example, we may identify ourselves as mild-mannered and easy-going, and yet there may be another (secret) part of us, residing in the shadow, that is filled with anger and a propensity for violence. Normally this part is well hidden from ourselves and others.[9] Occasionally, it may jump out and surprise us. When this happens, we may apologetically say, "That wasn't me!" or "I wasn't myself."

Ad agencies, screenwriters, and authors know these hidden parts very well and may skillfully manipulate our thoughts and feelings with certain words and images. This is one reason we see so many movies, TV shows, books, and magazines filled with images of sex and violence. These stories may appeal to the shadow side without forcing us to acknowledge these same feelings within ourselves.

These hidden conflicts can surface in several arenas of our lives. A frequent battleground for conflict is the body. Muscle tension, headaches, upset stomachs, and various stress-related ailments are usually symptoms of an inner war occurring. An injury or illness is often the result of a battle raging within us.

In 1971 I began to experience some severe headaches that had no identifiable physical cause. After visiting many medical doctors—including specialists of every variety—I found no relief whatever. The pain grew more severe. At the end of 1972, I was forced to consider a medical leave from my work. I was frustrated and frightened.

Early in 1973, through a very unusual sequence of events, I was led (with great reluctance) to a meditation group. Had it not been for my desperation, I would not have even considered such an "irrational" activity. But I gave it a try.

Like Alice in Wonderland, I discovered a whole new world; actually, it was a whole new universe. I became aware of an inner conflict about my suppressed spirituality. I was raised Roman Catholic and left the Church at age twenty. My father was a fundamentalist Christian and very critical of my Catholic education. In 1971 I was a strident agnostic, a secular humanist. I was suppressing my own spirituality, which was seeking to be expressed. This created an inner conflict. Since I was not consciously aware of this inner conflict, it appeared in the form of a headache.

The meditation practice provided the foundation for my body/soul healing. Someone in the group introduced me to Unity. Within a period of one year, I was living in a world that I never before knew existed. That year—and those headaches—radically altered the course of my life. Because I had been suppressing the pain connected with my early spiritual life, I had also been suppressing my own spirituality and ignoring the call to explore this part of my being.

Another battleground for our inner conflicts may be our personal relationships. When others "push our buttons" it's a sure sign they are calling up the battles that are already taking place within us. Other people become mirrors for some hidden part of ourselves. This is especially so with our intimate relationships. This principle also applies to collective relationships, such as those between nations and cultures. Every nation is a large family system. The battlegrounds within us may become external battlegrounds with real people suffering and dying.

Our bodies, our relationships, or our finances may become mirrors for the parts of us that we have hidden from ourselves. What we do not see directly, within ourselves, will show up in our bodies or environments. Our lives provide every opportunity we need to meet and to reconcile the conflicts within us.

If we are judging or condemning someone or something else, then we are most likely (unconsciously) judging or condemning some part of ourselves that is being projected onto the other. If we have an inordinate degree of fear about something, it may reflect something within ourselves that frightens us. And if we have an excessive amount of adulation for someone else, we may be projecting onto him or her some disowned positive quality of our own. The essence of psychological projection is that we do not see a particular quality within ourselves, so we ascribe it to someone else and then react as if it were *all* about them.

When I was younger, I had strong judgments about anyone I perceived to be arrogant. I identified myself as modest and humble because I was taught that these were "good" qualities and that arrogance was "bad." Years later I discovered a (heretofore) hidden part of myself which was highly arrogant and which felt superior to others. Once I learned to accept that part of myself, I found that so-called arrogant people no longer annoyed me. (Now I see them as "spunky.")

Accepting a part of ourselves does not necessarily mean that we accept its viewpoint as truth. It simply means that we make room for all those parts of ourselves, whether they seem to make sense or not. Every child (inner and outer) deserves to be loved—no matter how distorted his picture of reality may seem to our adult minds.

Certainly, we continue to use discernment and sound judgment when necessary, but we see that sound judgment is rarely accompanied by feelings of condemnation and criticism. We can identify what is unwise or harmful without the need to condemn the perpetrators of such acts. We can avoid harmful or toxic persons, places, and things without condemnation. We can love all beings yet not "pet the rattlesnakes." Love and acceptance don't preclude the need to avoid what may be harmful to us.

The Self, the Individuality, transcends the opposites that comprise the human personality. The personality sees with the eyes of duality, because it sees projections of its own dualistic nature. The Self sees only oneness, because it is whole, undivided, in integrity with itself. This Self is the force that will heal the conflict of opposites within us.

A fable tells of a time when the Sun heard tales of great darkness upon Earth. After hearing these stories many times, he decided to find out for himself. He came to Earth and walked to and fro across the entire planet. He could not find any darkness.

The personality sees healing as the elimination of the "bad" side of the conflict. The so-called bad side may be perceived within ourselves or within another person. "If only I could get rid of this negative emotion." "If only this person would change." The personality is always identified with one side of the conflict. It sees with limited vision—at best, only half the picture.

The Individuality sees that all conflict is as two ends of the same rope. You can cut off the "bad end" and you will still have two different ends. You can saw off the negative end of a magnet and you will still have a positive and negative end. You can try to get rid of every bad person outside of you or every bad trait within you and he or she or it will show up somewhere else in a different form. The Individuality knows this because it is whole. The personality doesn't, because it is fragmented.

All healing is the transcendence of opposites. Wholeness is the product of balancing, reconciling, and integrating opposites. Please note that we are not talking about the destruction of opposites. That is not possible. The rope always has two ends. Healing occurs when we see that both ends *belong to the same rope.*

Opposites are necessary for the creative process. But the process may become destructive when we believe that the opposites are intrinsically different rather than opposite poles of the same underlying reality. Male and female are creative opposites. *Vive la différence!* But when we fail to see the underlying human connection transcending gender, we have relationships that are fraught with conflict. The same is true in the relationships among races and nations. When we fail to see the underlying oneness of all humanity, we live in a world of perpetual conflict.

A story from India tells of two rival families of frogs—one green and one yellow—living in separate wells about one hundred feet apart. At night the frogs would sit on the edge of their respective wells hurtling insults and threats at one another. Each considered the other an intractable enemy. One day it was very hot so a green frog swam unusually deep in search of cool water. He swam a long way in his quest. Upon returning to the surface, he found himself in the yellow frogs' well! At that moment he saw through the illusion of their perceived separateness. He returned to his own well to share the news of their essential similarity with the yellow frogs. (The story doesn't tell us how successful he was in convincing his compatriots.)

We tend to see opposites as irreconcilably different,

Illustration 1.

mutually exclusive, and very far apart. [See Illustration 1.] In the Chinese philosophy of Taoism, opposites are seen from a perspective very different from our traditional Western view. In Taoism, opposites are seen to be complementary parts of a greater whole. These opposites are referred to as *yin* and *yang*. The symbol depicting the relationship between yin and yang is called the *tai chi*, meaning "the great ultimate." [See Illustration 2.] The illustration shows us that these opposing energies are part of a larger unity. Together they form complete wholeness. The energies of yin and yang are opposites, yet they are not in conflict. Their relationship is more of a dance than a battle. The two smaller circles depict the principle that the seeds of each side are contained within its opposite. In Chinese medicine, healing is seen to be the result of the proper relationship, the right balance, between the two energies.

As an example, let's look at the apparent opposites of life and death. In the Western view, we see them as

Illustration 2.

very different, in opposition to each other, and mutually exclusive. From the Taoist perspective, this relationship is seen differently. Life and death are seen to be parts of a greater wholeness. Life and death interrelate with one another. The seeds of each are contained within the other.

Nature seems to reflect this view. In nature, life and death are virtually inseparable; they are both part of the cycle of nature. The fruit rots that the seed may be nourished. The seed dies that the seedling may sprout. The seedling is nurtured by the compost of dead vegetation. "Unless a grain of wheat falls into the earth and dies, it remains alone; but if it dies, it bears much fruit" (Jn. 12:24). Nature does not resist death or cling to life as do most humans. Nature knows that life and death are but different phases of the same cycle, different ends of the same rope, and both are necessary for nature's state of wholeness.

Individuation, the movement toward wholeness, is the process of reconciling opposites into a greater unity. Perhaps it would be more correct to say that it's the process of seeing that, in reality, apparent opposites are *already* part of a greater unity. Wholeness is seeing through the eyes of oneness rather than duality and then living our lives in congruence with this vision of oneness. This might be what Jesus meant when he referred to the "kingdom of heaven." In the *Gospel of Thomas* is recorded:

> They said to Him: "Shall we then, being children, enter the Kingdom?" Jesus said

to them: "When you make the two one, and
when you make the inner as the outer and
the outer as the inner and the above as the
below, and when you make the male and the
female into a single one, then you shall enter
the Kingdom."[10]

Wholeness is much broader and deeper than our conditioned concept of perfection. The traditional Christian teaching has been to strive toward some image
of perfection rather than to engage in the quest for
wholeness. Robert Johnson writes:

Perfection suggests something all pure with
no blemishes, dark spots, or questionable
areas. Wholeness includes even the darkness
but combines the dark elements with the light
elements into a totality. Generally speaking,
the Christian striving has been toward goodness and perfection, not toward wholeness
and completion. The movement toward
wholeness is a formidable task, for it always
involves us in paradox.[11]

The movement toward wholeness always involves us
in paradox. Our conditioned view is that things have
to be "one way or another," either "this or that." Wholeness means living from the ground of Being that includes and transcends "this or that."

The personality cannot see beyond the divisions that
it creates. The ego must surrender to the Self, the divine
within, in order to move beyond the limitation of sepa-

ration. Every time the Self is experienced, the ego is defeated.

Conflict as Opportunity

Wholeness evolves from the reconciliation of opposites. This process is essential for individuation. We must first become aware of these opposites within us before they can be reconciled. This often occurs through our awareness of some conflict (internal or external) in our lives. Awareness of conflict is often the first step toward individuation.

Many of us are conditioned to believe that conflict is bad. We may attempt to avoid it because of our belief that it is impolite, dangerous, or sinful. When conflict arises, we may rush in with medication, meditation, or mediation in an attempt to quell it as quickly as possible. Each of these practices can be a force for healing if used wisely, or each one can be used as a "whitewash" to suppress awareness of internal conflicts that need to be acknowledged.

If we suppress symptoms of disease or conflict, we may inhibit the process of healing. By attending to the symptoms with an open mind and an open heart, we take a great step toward wholeness. Marilyn Ferguson writes: "Conflict, pain, tension, fear, paradox . . . these are transformations trying to happen. Once we confront them, the transformative process begins."[12]

The word *confront* is derived from a French word that essentially means "face to face." We must come face to face with our problems and our conflicts for individuation to proceed.

Most recovering alcoholics are recovering only because they have acknowledged, "I am an alcoholic." This statement is made not as an affirmation of one's true identity but rather as an acknowledgment of the existence of a problem. Once we confront a problem, the transformative process begins.

This is not to encourage anyone to create conflict for its own sake. Although many folks dislike conflict and seek to avoid it, some people secretly enjoy conflict, chaos, and turmoil. They may find a certain sense of excitement, familiarity, or distraction in such conflict. Here, external conflict is used as a means of hiding from a deeper, internal conflict. Conflict, like suffering, has no value in itself, other than the opportunity it may provide to enter into a deep healing.

Much of our challenge with conflict arises from the belief that "it shouldn't be happening." We see conflict as something wrong and we seek to right that wrong. Yet if we look at the natural world, we see that it's full of conflict. Animals are in conflict with other animals over food and territory. Plants are in conflict with other plants over soil and sunlight. The sea is in conflict with the rocky shoreline. The wind is in conflict with the sea. Earth is constantly in conflict with itself.

Nature does not view conflict as wrong. Nature does not view conflict as a contest of good vs. bad, right vs. wrong, righteous vs. unrighteous. Nature does not attempt to permanently destroy the bad, the wrong, the unrighteous as humans often do. Nature accepts conflict as the natural interaction of opposing forces.

Author Gregg Levoy writes:

> Friction is a fundamental property of nature and nothing grows without it—not mountains, not pearls, not people. It is precisely the quality of fragility . . . the capacity for being "shaken up," that is paradoxically the key to growth. Any structure—whether at the molecular, chemical, physical, social, or psychological level—that is insulated from disturbance is also protected from change. It becomes stagnant.[13]

The first step in healing conflict is to see it not as wrong but to see it as the natural consequence of opposing forces interacting with one another. The next step is to become intimately acquainted with both sides of the conflict. We are typically identified with only one side. As stated earlier, one or both sides of the conflict are usually unconscious.

If both sides are unconscious, we usually feel the symptoms of the conflict (or our resistance to it) but don't understand what the conflict is about. We may simply feel tension or anxiety or anger and not know why. If one side is conscious, then we usually identify with that side (I am that person) and deny or project the other side (I am not that person).

For example, I might project the unconscious side

onto another person or other people. (You know whom I mean—that person from hell, sent here only to torment you!) Or I may experience the other side as some evil force within that is bent on my undoing. This force may appear in the form of a physical ailment, an addiction, behavior disorder, or some emotional disturbance.

Our work is to become acquainted with these hidden parts of ourselves. The first step in the process is not to run away from the conflict or tension but to be willing to face it. Recognize that conflict is simply the natural consequence of opposing forces interacting. And know that the Self, our own spiritual nature, is there to guide us through the process and bring us home to Itself.

The next step is to recognize that both the source and the solution to the conflict lie within you. This may be fairly obvious if the issue is a physical disease or some internal disorder. If the conflict is with another person or with circumstances outside of you, it may not be so obvious.

Does this mean you're always the one who is wrong? No. It means that the source and the solution to the conflict always lie within you. It is not a matter of right or wrong. Seeing the situation in the dualism of right-wrong or good-bad keeps us entangled in our personality issues, our self-created dramas that take us nowhere, except into more conflict.

No matter what occurs in my external world, it isn't a problem until it upsets me. A problem, by definition, is something that triggers something within me that I perceive as unacceptable. When we experience some feeling judged as unacceptable, we then label that event which triggered the feeling as unacceptable. For example, if a friend is twenty minutes late for an appointment, I may or may not find that a problem. It's a problem if it upsets me. It's not a problem if it doesn't.

Attempting to change another's behavior is a different issue altogether. It may be appropriate to ask our friends to be more punctual or tell them that the next time we'll wait no more than ten minutes. I can do this without making them wrong or becoming upset. If I am upset, then it is my problem, and the cure for that problem is within me.

We listen to both sides of our conflict not from a "right or wrong" attitude but from the perspective of seeing two opposing forces meeting each other. We acknowledge this as an opportunity for greater self-awareness and for healing. This attitude is the foundation of some methods of psychotherapy.

Joel, forty-six years old, was divorced by his homemaker wife after a twelve-year marriage. Accustomed to intimacy and a supportive woman, he felt surprised at the strength of his attraction to Ellen, a stockbroker, who clearly thrived in her autonomy. During their first six months of dating, they did a dance: he pulled her in, while she pushed him away.

As the relationship progressed, Joel did not wish to face his separateness and tried to feel safe through fusion with Ellen. In response, she created a shield and clung to her separateness for safety, judging his dependency needs (as well as her own) as unacceptable. Whereas he feared abandonment most of all, she feared being overwhelmed by his neediness.

Their relationship soon became problematic. Joel felt that he could never get enough love from Ellen. Ellen felt smothered. Finally, she lashed out at Joel with cruel words, cutting their intimacy in an effort to restore her own sense of safety. This pattern returned many times. The relationship was in crisis.

With the help of their therapist, they discovered the hidden characters at work in the relationship: the fuser and the distancer. They found that this pair of opposites had been split between them, each displaying both qualities. They were "shadowboxing" with one another. Their work involved making each of them conscious of his or her disowned traits. As Joel slowly learned to overcome his fear of being alone and found an authentic sense of security within himself, he began to uncover a shadow character that held his need for healthful separateness. He gradually grew to enjoy solitude.

As Ellen allowed herself to feel loved, she began to feel more emotionally dependent on Joel, even to need him, uncovering a shadow character that held her own need for intimacy. She was deeply afraid of these vulnerable feelings, which she had repressed for a long time.

With ongoing therapy, they continued to bring more of themselves into conscious awareness and thus opened new avenues of intimacy. Eventually, the two discovered together that Ellen's fear of fusion was just the other side of Joel's fear of abandonment.[14]

Techniques for Self-Awareness and Healing

If one side of the conflict is hidden (which it usually is), we may employ certain techniques and practices to aid in our discovery of this unconscious element. Meditation and self-observation are always recommended and form the foundation for all other practices.

Journaling is also helpful for many people. This is a process of recording one's thoughts and feelings in a personal journal on a regular basis. There are many systems of journaling. The essential element in most systems of journaling is to write from your feeling nature rather than from the rational, thinking mind. Write how you feel, not what you think. This will tend to open you to new insights and understandings. The rational mind tends to think it already has it all figured out! When you first start to journal, you may not notice any specific results, but as you continue on a regular basis, you will gradually open deeper and deeper levels of awareness and insight.

If you are aware of a conflict, then journal from both sides of that conflict. When journaling from a particular side, let that personality element have "the floor" and say whatever it wants without interruption. Write it all down. Then do the same for the other side. For example, if you are working with an eating issue, let the hungry, impulsive part "speak" whatever it has to say. When it is finished, let the controlling or critical part speak as well. Record all of it. Dialogue between the two if you wish.

Dialogue work is similar to journaling and can also be very powerful. To dialogue is to allow a particular emotion or part of yourself to speak. Voice dialogue is a process of stating aloud what we are secretly, and often unconsciously, saying to ourselves internally. If working with a disease or physical ailment, we can give the disease or the affected body part a voice. If working with a relationship challenge, we can have (our version of) the other person speak from within ourselves.

If you feel in conflict with some part of yourself, let that part have a voice. For example, if you are depressed, become deeply aware of the feeling and then let it speak. You can do this verbally or in writing. Don't talk about the feeling, but let the feeling itself form the words. This is very important. You can do the same with an illness, a relationship, a problem of almost any nature. First, get deeply in touch with the perceived problem at the feeling level, and then give it a voice.

In the journaling or dialogue process, we can also respond to the "voice" from the other side of the conflict; thus a true dialogue ensues. You can respond to the voice and ask it questions. You might ask questions such as "What do you need?" "What gift do you have to give me?" Avoid analytical questions or statements such as "Explain why this is happening to me." Stay at the feeling level. If used skillfully and regularly, this practice can lead to deep healing and insights.

Imagery work is often useful. This is similar to the voice dialogue process, only instead of a voice, we allow a spontaneous image to arise in the awareness. It is particularly helpful when feeling strong emotions, stress, or pain in the body. If working with an emotion or a desire, become aware of the feeling or the desire and then allow it to give you an image. The image must come from the feeling, not from the rational mind. You can draw, paint, or sculpt the image. You can interact with the image through the dialogue process—either voice dialogue or journaling.

Dream work can be very productive. Carl Jung used this method extensively. (He analyzed more than 60,000 dreams in his professional practice.) The essential element in dream work is to remember one's dreams and to know that everything in the dream is part of the dreamer. Journaling the dream and dialoguing with some of the dream elements can be very fruitful. It is not necessary, or helpful, to intellectually dissect or analyze the dream. Stay with your feelings; trust your intuition. The dream will, in time, reveal its own meaning.

Psychotherapy can be very helpful. To seek help from a psychotherapist or counselor doesn't have to mean that you're mentally ill; it only means that you want some professional help in your journey to wholeness. And, as always, meditation and prayer form the foundation for our healing journeys. Working at all levels—physical, mental, and spiritual—is usually the best approach to healing.

The purpose of each of these processes is to reveal that which is hidden and then to reconcile and integrate that formerly fragmented and conflicting part into our personality in a functional and effectual way. As opposites within the psyche are reconciled, our identity gradually shifts from the personality to the Self. This is the process of individuation. This is the journey to wholeness.

Mile Markers

- The Self is the archetype of wholeness within every human being. It is both the source and the goal of human life.

- The Self is our Individuality. It is unique and indivisible. It is our essential nature.

- Individuation is the process of discovering and manifesting the Self—the archetype of wholeness. The process involves reconciling opposites, including uniqueness and sameness.

- The personality sees with a dualistic vision and sees a world of conflict. The Self, the Individuality, sees only oneness, unity, harmony.

- All spiritual healing involves the transcendence of opposites. Wholeness develops from balancing, reconciling, integrating opposites within ourselves.

- Conflict is an opportunity for healing. The first step is to see conflict as natural.

- The next step in healing conflict is to become intimately acquainted with both sides of the conflict. Usually, one side is hidden from our awareness.

- The next step is to realize that the source and the solution to all conflict lie within ourselves.

- Techniques for self-awareness and healing include journaling, dialogue, imagery, dream work, prayer/meditation, and self-observation.

Chapter Three Notes

1. Marie-Louise von Franz, *Carl Gustav Jung*, as quoted in Peter O'Connor, *Understanding Jung, Understanding Yourself* (New York: Paulist Press, 1985), p. 70.
2. Johnson uses the term *personality*. I have substituted the word *psyche* because, in the Jungian use of the word, it means the same. I will be using the term *personality* to mean something very different from the Jungian use.
3. Robert A. Johnson, *Transformation* (New York: HarperSanFrancisco, 1991), p. 84.
4. O'Connor, pp. 70–1.
5. T. S. Eliot as quoted in Robert Brumet, *Finding Yourself in Transition* (Unity Village, Missouri: Unity Books, 1995), p. 143.
6. Robert A. Johnson, *He: Understanding Masculine Psychology* (New York: Harper & Row, 1977), pp. 2–5.
7. Jung used the term *unconscious.*
8. At the personality level, we *are* the drama. This is our perceived identity.
9. It may not be as well hidden from others as we think! It's just that our friends may be too polite to tell us what we don't want to hear.
10. The Gospel of St. Thomas as quoted in Ken Wilber, *No Boundary* (Boston: Shambhala, 1981), p. 28.
11. Johnson, p. 63.
12. Marilyn Ferguson, *The Aquarian Conspiracy* (Los Angeles: J. P. Tarcher, Inc., 1980), p. 76.

13. Gregg Levoy, *Callings: Finding and Following an Authentic Life* (New York: Three Rivers Press, 1998), p. 8.

14. Connie Zweig and Steve Wolf, *Romancing the Shadow* (New York: Ballantine Books, 1997), pp. 150–1.

Adventure Three

Individuation: Discovering Your Wholeness

The I Am is the same in all men and all women.
It is without limit in its capacity to express the
potentialities of God.

—Charles Fillmore[1]

The Self is the archetype of wholeness. The Self is our Individuality, the I Am. It is the goal of individuation. Individuation is the process of shifting our primary identification from the personality to the Self.

The Self is who we really are. The personality is who we think we are. Our level of wholeness depends upon how strongly we are identified with the Self—the I Am— rather than the personality. We do not lose our personalities; our personalities become richer because they then function as vehicles for the Self. All aspects of the personality are illumined with the light of Self.

Before the time of Copernicus most people thought Earth to be the center of the universe. The Sun was seen as one of many celestial bodies orbiting the

---

[1] Charles Fillmore, *Keep a True Lent* (Unity Village, Missouri: Unity Books, 1995), pp. 56–7.

Earth. Copernicus introduced a paradigm shift. Since his time, the Sun is seen as the center of our solar system, with Earth orbiting it. When we experience a paradigm shift in consciousness, the Self, not the personality, becomes the center of our lives. We let the personality "orbit" the Self. We then experience a state of wholeness, wherein we see beyond the dualistic vision of the personality. We see with new eyes. The oneness of all life is revealed to us.

Soul–Talk

I am one with the Source of all life. I am whole.

Write this declaration three times, pausing between each line to allow the statement to saturate your consciousness. Then say it aloud or silently as often as possible each day.

1. _____

2. _____

3. _____

Soul-Thoughts

 After you have completed writing your Soul-Talk, take time to sit quietly and observe your thoughts and feelings. Write them down.

 1. In your everyday life, how do you determine if you are functioning from Self (Individuality) or from personality? What are the indicators?

 2. Describe a time when you were caught up in personality. What were the indicators? What was the result?

3. Describe a time when you were functioning from the Self, the Individuality. What were the indicators? What was the result?

4. Describe a time when you fostered a healing in yourself or in a relationship by seeing beyond apparent opposites.

5. What techniques do you most often use for self-awareness and healing? Why have you selected these particular techniques?

Off the Main Trail

Use a technique such as journaling, dialogue, or imagery to work with a current conflict or experience of suffering in your life.

Stepping-Stone

 Practice self-observation and keep a journal of your daily experiences. Notice when you experience conflict (inner or outer) and when you are able to see beyond conflict to the underlying wholeness. Pay attention to what brings about the shift from one view to another.

I am one with the Source of all life. I am whole.

Chapter Four

Spiritual Alchemy: The Transformation of Suffering

> There is no such thing as a problem
> without a gift for you in its hands.
> —Richard Bach[1]

During medieval times, researchers known as alchemists sought a secret process that they believed would turn base metals, such as lead, into gold. A few of these alchemists, however, were seeking something much more profound. These researchers were studying the processes whereby our base human consciousness could be transformed into a "golden" spiritual consciousness. They saw that human life is the laboratory wherein this process takes place. And they saw that every human challenge is an opportunity for converting the lead of our human personality into the gold of our spiritual essence. We will see that every experience of suffering is an opportunity for transformation. Each one of us can be an alchemist.

The First Step in Spiritual Healing

The first step in spiritual healing is to recognize our own needs for healing. With physical illness these needs may seem obvious. In other situations the needs may not be so obvious. Some conditions of suffering seem to involve other persons or external circumstances. If we are blaming other persons or circumstances for our suffering, then we are not seeing the need for our own spiritual healing. Spiritual healing begins with the recognition that "I'm the one who needs to be healed." The alchemical process begins with us.

Spiritual healing begins when we are willing to be changed. It will not occur if we want others to change or if we want circumstances to change, but are not willing to change ourselves. Other people in our lives may need healing as much as we do, but we will never become whole if we focus on their need for healing instead of our own.

Spiritual healing is a healing of consciousness. A spiritual healing may cause circumstances to change, but the true healing is the healing of our consciousness, not just the change of external conditions. Healing occurs when we realize the Truth beyond all appearances. Healing of consciousness is releasing error in our minds and awakening to Truth. This will occur only after we acknowledge the need for healing our own consciousness.

Spiritual healing begins as we turn to God for help. We turn to God first because our original nature is spiritual. As spiritual beings, we are expressions of God, never separated from our Source. We are spiritual beings having human experiences. The true solution to every human problem lies in the discovery of our spiritual nature.

Bill Wilson, one of the founders of Alcoholics Anonymous, was informed by Carl Jung that the only permanent solution to alcoholism was to experience "union with God."[2] In a letter to Wilson, Dr. Jung explained that the alcoholic's craving for alcohol is a misplaced spiritual thirst for wholeness. He quoted the 42d Psalm: "As a hart longs for flowing streams, so longs my soul for thee, O God. My soul thirsts for God, for the living God."

We turn to God first and then to human beings as God guides us. Turning to God for help does not necessarily mean that we avoid human assistance. It does not mean that we refuse to change harmful conditions in our lives. We may need to turn to God for help *and* move our feet. God works through us but not for us. God is not a giant in the sky who will solve our problems for us, but God is that Giant within us who will guide us to right understanding and to right action.

Turning to human help or avoiding a harmful condition should not be a substitute for healing our consciousness, but sometimes it may be a prerequisite for the healing of consciousness. Sometimes conditions of suffering are so intense that it may be difficult to focus on our internal healing until some external relief is found. And if a person is addicted to a harmful substance

or behavior, the initial focus may need to be on absten-
tion and behavior modification before the deeper healing can occur.

Creating the Healing Vision

Any condition of suffering—physical, mental, emotional, or spiritual—is a condition of disease (dis-ease).
We define *disease* as "any departure from wholeness;
any harmful or destructive condition; any condition
of suffering." We begin the spiritual healing process
by acknowledging our own needs for healing and then
turning to God for help. The next step is to look at our
responses to the experience of disease. Often our initial response is "Something is wrong; this shouldn't be
happening!" We may feel resistance and anger. We
protest. "Why did this happen to me?" "Why now?" "I
did all the right things and now this happens; it's not
fair!"

We usually view our suffering as something that happens *to* us. It may appear that we've become victims of
some unwanted force disrupting our lives, liberty, and
pursuit of happiness. We are conditioned to believe
that we are in control of our lives. When something
unpleasant happens that seems beyond our control,
we may feel like victims of some "evil power."

If you should find yourself responding in this way,
do not become self-critical. That will only increase your
suffering. Responding to a major disease with denial,
anger, or guilt is very common. These responses are
ways that we defend ourselves against the more vulnerable feelings of intense fear or grief.

We need to recognize and honestly acknowledge our responses to the condition without guilt or apology. We must have compassion for ourselves or else we add to our suffering. After becoming aware of and accepting our initial responses, we may then ask ourselves, "Is there another way to see this?" Often we respond to a disease the same way we would respond to a flat tire: "Let's get it fixed so that I can get on with my life." We may see suffering as a major inconvenience that is getting in the way of our plans. We usually see a disease as a "stumbling block," as something that blocks our conscious desires and intentions. Spiritual healing begins when we are willing to see our suffering as a stepping-stone rather than as a stumbling block. Healing begins when we can open ourselves to the possibility of a hidden gift within the suffering. There is no such thing as a problem without a gift for you in its hands.

An oyster's first experience of a pearl is that of an irritating grain of sand which shouldn't be there. Just as the pearl forms from an irritant in the oyster, we can discover great pearls of wisdom from those conditions that irritate us. The potential wisdom is already within us, but it may take an irritant to bring it forth. In dealing with our irritants skillfully, we discover something within us that we never before could see. Who would believe that the lowly oyster could produce such a great prize as the pearl? Within us lies the potential for the "pearl of great price." This pearl is the priceless wisdom, power, and freedom for which we would gladly have given all our possessions.

Jean Houston writes:

> In times of suffering, when you feel aban-
> doned, perhaps even annihilated, there is
> occurring—at levels deeper than your pain—
> the entry of the sacred, the possibility of re-
> demption. Wounding opens the doors of our
> sensibility to a larger reality, which is blocked
> by our habituated and conditioned point of
> view . . . . Pathos gives us eyes and ears to see
> and hear what our normal eyes and ears
> cannot.[3]

We should not expect ourselves to be happy when
we experience suffering. We honor our human response
to the situation and then open ourselves to the possibility of a spiritual gift within the suffering. Our human
personalities would not choose this condition, and we
would probably like it to go away. Yet we can consider
the possibility of an Inner Wisdom at work in our lives,
and we can learn to trust that Wisdom.

The Old Testament character Job suffered so much
that he lamented the day he was born. He questioned
God and asserted his own self-righteousness. He finally
woke up when the Lord spoke to him and asked him
this question: "Where were you when I laid the foundation of the earth?" (Job 38:4) Job recognized the inadequacy of his limited human understanding. He responded: "I had heard of thee by the hearing of the ear,
but now my eye sees thee . . ." (Job 42:5). Job finally
saw God at work within his suffering—not just in the-

ory but in direct experience: "Now my eye sees thee . . . ."
Job's ability to see God at work in spite of the negative
conditions in his life opened him to the possibility of
healing. "And the Lord restored the fortunes of Job . . .
and the Lord gave Job twice as much as he had before"
(Job 42:10).

Spiritual healing begins with the recognition of a need
for healing, a willingness to turn to God for help, and
a willingness to believe that in some way our suffering
may be a blessing in disguise. Our human understanding may not be able to comprehend the purpose of our
conditions. Yet if we are open to the possibility of some
wisdom at work beyond our human understanding,
we have opened the door for our spiritual healing.
When we consider our suffering as an opportunity for
a deeper awareness of our true spiritual nature, we
may get a glimpse of the gift that lies before us. That
gift is always a greater degree of wholeness.

How can suffering—dis-ease—open us to a deeper
experience of our spiritual nature? We are essentially
spiritual beings. Our inherent nature is perfect wholeness. Our inherent nature is thus because we are,
in reality, individualized expressions of God, which is
wholeness itself. In our human experience, we unknowingly abandon this awareness of our true nature
and live in the dreamlike awareness of the human mind
and the human senses. Suffering gives us an opportunity to awaken from the dream of the human mind to
the reality of Divine Mind. This is spiritual alchemy.

Author Kat Duff suffered from a debilitating illness

for two years. During her illness, she once had to turn down an invitation to participate in a meditation retreat because she didn't feel up to sitting for hours on end. She felt disheartened, wondering when she'd feel well enough to resume spiritual practice. As she was falling asleep that night, however, she suddenly understood that her illness *was* her spiritual practice, an opportunity to meditate, a way to employ the alchemical art of turning lead into gold. She writes:

> I've come to see that I contact "the divine," or it comes forward most clearly to me, when I'm in my most human limitedness, whereas before I was seeking it by trying to be godlike, trying to transcend my humanness. It's an immense comfort to me that I'm closest to the divine by being closest to my own humanness and vulnerability.[4]

Ironically, we are able to see beyond our humanness when we allow ourselves to be fully human. We embrace our divinity by fully embracing our humanity, even though our humanity may seem very limited and vulnerable.

Our human level of awareness is not bad; it is simply incomplete and inaccurate. Through human awareness alone, we grasp only a partial and distorted view of reality. When we believe that this partial view is the only reality, then we are lost, missing the mark, living in a "fallen state." The condition of suffering is a symptom of living in this alienated state. Suffering is not punishment, but is a natural consequence of living in the experience of separation from our Source. Like a symptom of physical disease, the existence of suffering is a reminder that we have not realized our true nature. Suffering shows us that we are in conflict with ourselves—that we are not yet whole and have not integrated all the opposites within the personality.

The ego believes that it has the answers, that it knows the truth, and that it is in control. When we adopt the attitude of a learner, being willing to humble ourselves as a child, we begin to see our dis-ease as stepping-stones to greater freedom. "Whoever humbles himself like this child, he is the greatest in the kingdom of heaven" (Mt. 18:4), the Master told his disciples. In the condition of suffering, we are humbled. We realize that we don't have the answers and that we aren't in control. At this point we can become open, childlike, willing to be taught by life. If we can do this and let go of our expectations of how things should be, the apparent obstacles in our paths begin to transform themselves. But if we assert the ego and live from fear, anger, and resistance, we fail to see the gift within the apparent obstacle.

> Shiva and Shakti, the Divine Couple in Hinduism, are in their heavenly abode watching over the earth. They are touched by the challenges of human life, the complexity of human reactions, and the ever-present place of suffering in the human experience. As

they watch, Shakti spies a miserably poor man walking down a road. His clothes are shabby and his sandals are tied together with rope. Her heart is wrung with compassion. Touched by his goodness and his struggle, Shakti turns to her divine husband and begs him to give this man some gold. Shiva looks at the man for a long moment. "My Dearest Wife," he says, "I cannot do that." Shakti is astounded, "Why, what do you mean, Husband? You are Lord of the Universe. Why can't you do this simple thing?"

"I cannot give this to him because he is not yet ready to receive it," Shiva replies. Shakti becomes angry. "Do you mean to say that you cannot drop a bag of gold in his path?"

"Surely I can," Shiva replies, "but that is quite another thing."

"Please, Husband," says Shakti.

And so Shiva drops a bag of gold in the man's path.

The man meanwhile walks along thinking to himself, "I wonder if I will find dinner tonight—or shall I go hungry again?" Turning a bend in the road, he sees something on the path in his way. "Aha," he says. "Look there, a large rock. How fortunate that I have seen it. I might have torn these poor

sandals of mine even further." And carefully
stepping over the bag of gold, he goes on his
way.[5]

Because of our habituated way of seeing, we may
fail to recognize that the very thing we try to avoid is
a "bag of gold" in disguise. This story was told to Dr.
Rachel Naomi Remen by a cancer patient, himself a
physician. She asked him if Life had ever dropped him
a bag of gold that he recognized and used to enrich his
life. "Cancer," he said simply.[6]

The bag of gold in your path may be that which you
perceive as the biggest obstacle in your life. "Resist not
evil" (Mt. 5:39 KJV), Jesus taught the multitude. These
three words contain a mountain of wisdom. We usually perceive "evil" to be something that can harm us
in some way. When we experience an obstacle such as
cancer, depression, or divorce, we often meet it with
resistance. We want it to go away. We see it as an evil
intruder in our lives. Meeting the experiences of our
lives with nonresistance is a way to begin seeing God
at work in every event in our lives. This leads us to the
gold hidden within the obstacle.

When we resist evil, we see life with a dualistic vision.
This creates an attitude of conflict and aggression. To
allow the appearance of evil, with no resistance, is to
deny its power. To deny the power of evil is to under-
mine our belief in its reality. We resist what we believe
is real; we don't resist that which we know is not. When
we deny the reality of evil, then we see God at work in

all persons, all things, and all events. Unity author
Imelda Shanklin writes:

> The essence of nonresistance is unity. You are
> not isolated from the rest of the universe. You
> are an indispensable part of the universe, and
> as such the universe loves, protects, and cher-
> ishes you. In so caring for you the universe is
> self-preserving.[7]

Nonresistance is an internal stance, an attitude,
rather than a formula for behavior. Nonresistance does
not mean that we refuse treatment for a disease if that
seems the wise thing to do. It doesn't mean that we
don't protect ourselves or that we permit harmful events
to occur if we can avoid them. We can avoid that which
is harmful without resorting to condemnation and resistance. Nonresistance is cherishing ourselves as the
universe itself cherishes us.

When suffering occurs in our lives, it is wise to perceive it as a teacher rather than as an evil intruder.
Suffering is an opportunity to let go of an illusion and
come into a deeper realization of Truth. Only the person experiencing the disease can discover the specific
teaching within it, but always it's an opportunity for
greater freedom and wholeness. The true healing is not
simply the removal of external symptoms but the experience of greater wholeness. The spiritual teacher
Ram Dass writes: "Healing is not the same as curing,
after all; healing does not mean going back to the way

things were before, but rather allowing *what is now* to move us closer to God."[8]

If we are experiencing great suffering, or if our lives are threatened, then we may be more open to learning. Often the experience of disease provides the opportunity and the incentive to go deeper than we would otherwise go in our searches for spiritual understanding. Many people have discovered their spiritual paths only after being confronted with serious illness and, often, only when they have exhausted all conventional means for a cure. The healing story of Myrtle Fillmore (see Chapter One) is a classic example of this. Many people have discovered their spiritual paths through recovery from an addiction. Many have discovered meditation originally as a means to relieve stress or to control pain. Many have turned to God for help only when all conventional means have failed.

What appears as evil at one point in our lives may eventually be seen as God at work. This may be difficult to see when we're in the midst of our suffering. Yet divorce, addiction, illness, or the death of a spouse may be the very condition that nurtures a transformation far beyond our human understanding.

Psychologist Andrea Nelson writes about depression as a catalyst for transformation:

> A state of depression contains within it the potential for growth. When a depressed person is confronted with the turmoil of a life

crisis, she is, willingly or unwillingly, immersed in the far-from-equilibrium conditions that are ripe for a spontaneous shift to a higher level of integration. While she is destabilized psychologically and emotionally, a bifurcation point is reached in which her rigid way of ordering her world is shaken. Irresistible chaos erupts, and she may feel anchorless, panicky, or overwhelmed. If she is able to flow with these feelings and confront the chaos, she may evolve a more flexible and adaptive way of ordering her world.[9]

Dr. Nelson gives an example with a client named Brian who felt anxious, guilty, and consumed with self-blame when a significant love relationship ended. He initially coped with his feelings by frenetic activity at work. However, one day his boss yelled at him unfairly, which cast him into a deep depression and was the last straw that finally propelled him into therapy. He soon discovered in therapy that his recent loss rekindled feelings of shame, inadequacy, and a distorted, negative self-image which had begun in early childhood when he was severely abused. His current crisis involved an influx of intense emotional energy that catapulted Brian into a chaotic state—fertile ground for transformation:

> Brian's depression and inner turmoil were positive signs that his old pattern of psychological organization was breaking down. He had been trapped in an established order and

never questioned his negative view of himself. Psychotherapy involved helping Brian accept, face, and eventually understand the chaos of his emotional crisis. Therapy supported conditions that challenged his restricted and static sense of self in a way that was difficult for him to reject. This fresh input triggered an expansion of his sense of self, and he began to see the world and himself differently. However, he often felt anchorless and unable to connect with his habitual patterns of coping. He was frightened by this at times but was also encouraged to trust that this chaos could open new possibilities. As he began to integrate a more complexly organized and healthy self-image, he felt less damaged, and his sensitivity to criticism and rejection diminished. He felt less anxious and guilty, and he was able to initiate more meaningful relationships in his personal life and at work.[10]

We explore the symptom of suffering from the perspective that the malady itself is the pathway to awakening more fully to our true nature. We explore it not with an attitude of analysis or intellectual understanding but with an attitude of spiritual understanding. Seeing suffering as a teacher, we perceive it as a stepping-stone to greater wisdom and freedom, rather than an obstacle blocking our personal goals.

Gregg Levoy reflects this viewpoint as he talks about physical symptoms:

> Like dreams, body symptoms present information of which we're unconscious. In a dream, this information comes as symbols. In the body, it comes as symptoms. Both mean exactly the same thing: signs! Sickness is a dream in the body, and symptoms are possessed of what the physicist David Bohm calls "soma-significance." They mean something. They have wisdom, metaphoric power, method in their madness. They are one of the languages the soul uses to get across to us something about itself.[11]

"There is nothing to be healed, only something to be learned" is a statement that underscores a basic premise in spiritual healing. Seeing our disease or our suffering as an opportunity to learn, rather than a need to wage war against evil, opens us to the possibility of deep healing. This is an opportunity to open ourselves more fully to our divine nature. See it as an opportunity for growth rather than as a condition arising from some personal deficiency. Spiritual learning is an ongoing process that occurs at many levels and at various stages in our evolutions. We are constantly growing in our journey of awakening.

Crucifixion and Resurrection

One handbook for our journey is the Bible. We can discover many Truth principles through the study of the Bible, and particularly, the study of the life of Jesus. One of these principles is that "resurrection always follows crucifixion." Crucifixion symbolizes the "crossing out" of illusions held within the human personality. This crossing out can take many forms. It often takes the form of some type of disease, some form of suffering. Crucifixion does not inherently cause suffering. The crucifixion is in consciousness. Most of our suffering is caused by our resistance to the process, rather than by the process itself. Nevertheless, because our human personalities are generally identified with some illusion, crucifixions are seldom easy.

Crucifixion is only half of the picture; on the other side lies resurrection. It is largely our unawareness or lack of conviction in this principle that causes us to resist our crucifixions. "What the caterpillar calls the end of the world, the master calls a butterfly."[12] The vision of the caterpillar is the vision of the unenlightened human personality. The vision of the master is the vision of spiritual awareness. The personality sees only one side of the story; the Individuality (the undivided Self) sees the whole process.

The human personality is somewhat like a caterpillar. In the unawakened state our vision is earthbound and limited to the appearances before us. Like the caterpillar, we voraciously consume our environment, seeking to fill the never-ending hunger of the separate self. For the butterfly to be born, the caterpillar must die. Jesus refers to this principle when he says to his disciples: "He who finds his life will lose it, and he who loses his life for my sake will find it" (Mt. 10:39). This enigmatic statement refers to giving up or losing one's identification with the personality (the personal life) and then discovering and living from the Individuality, the Christ within (the universal life).

From the perspective of the butterfly we can rejoice, but when we are in the midst of the drama of crucifixion, holding this vision may be difficult. Trusting God in each moment is essential even if everything seems hopeless. This means not struggling with our feeling of hopelessness, but accepting that too, if it arises. Trust that *every* step is essential in your journey of healing and transformation.

The poet Rumi writes:

> This being human is a guest house
> Every morning a new arrival.
>
> A joy, a depression, a meanness,
> some momentary awareness comes
> as an unexpected visitor.
>
> Welcome and entertain them all!
> Even if they're a crowd of sorrows,
> who violently sweep your house
> empty of its furniture,

still, treat each guest honorably.
He may be clearing you out
for some new delight.

The dark thought, the shame, the malice,
meet them at the door laughing,
and invite them in.

Be grateful for whoever comes,
because each has been sent
as a guide from beyond.[13]

Our experiences of suffering can transform us if, instead of getting lost in fear, anger, and resistance, we can open ourselves to the possibility of resurrections on the other side of our crucifixions. This requires courage and a willingness to trust—to trust deeply.

Facing the hidden parts of ourselves is not easy. Very often dis-ease brings to the surface of our awareness a part of ourselves that we have buried deeply—buried because in the past facing it seemed too painful or difficult. But here it is before us, like it or not. As Marilyn Ferguson puts it: "Properly attended to, pain can answer our most crucial questions, even those we did not consciously frame. The only way out of our suffering is through it."[14]

When we pay attention to our suffering with open minds and with attitudes of nonresistance, we open ourselves to the possibility of being transformed by our experiences. The suffering itself will reveal its meaning to us, and from that meaning the new Self emerges. This is the resurrection.

The Shadow and the Blessing

Almost a century ago Dr. Carl Jung introduced the notion of the shadow as a psychological archetype. The shadow exists beneath our conscious awareness; it is the constellation of the rejected and despised parts of ourselves. We reject certain parts of ourselves because we have been conditioned to believe that these parts are evil or dangerous. Believing that we must banish these parts of self from existence, we pretend they don't exist . . . but they do. These buried parts of ourselves remain alive and find ways to crawl to the surface of our awareness.

One way that this happens is through various forms of disease—physical, emotional, behavioral, and relational. The experience of suffering is an opportunity to heal and to redeem these condemned and neglected parts of ourselves. Facing the suffering is facing ourselves. Facing the suffering with nonresistance is facing ourselves with kindness and compassion. Listening to the suffering is listening to the pain and confusion of the neglected self.

To pay attention is to look and to listen. To look and to listen is to discover the hidden gift within the apparent problem. "Reveal that which needs to be revealed" is a powerful prayer. To face all parts of ourselves with love and courage is to unleash the power of Spirit and to send it forth into our bodies, minds, and hearts to do its perfect work.

An example of this courage is given in a story of the Old Testament patriarch Jacob, who had a vision one night. In this vision he wrestled with a man until the breaking of the day and the man inflicted Jacob with a physical wound. As the two wrestled, the man said, "Let me go, for the day is breaking." Jacob replied, "I will not let you go, unless you bless me" (Gen. 32:26). The man said to him, "Your name shall no more be called Jacob, but Israel, for you have striven with God and with men, and have prevailed" (Gen. 32:28).

There are many pearls of wisdom in this story if we interpret it symbolically. We can liken Jacob's wrestling with the man to a condition of dis-ease—a state where we are wrestling with ourselves. We can see the wrestling as both the cause and the result of the condition of dis-ease. Suffering is the result of disharmony, a lack of balance within our body-mind systems. We can see it as one part of self struggling with another part.

Typically, at least one of these parts is within the subconscious mind—hidden from conscious awareness. (Note that Jacob wrestled with the man at night.) Conversely, suffering itself creates a certain amount of wrestling within our psyches. We may find ourselves in a state of emotional turmoil; we may experience conflicting feelings and desires. One part of us may have faith in God, while another part is frightened

and angry. Suffering may be both the cause and the
result of a struggle.

It's tempting to deny or resist our internal struggles.
However, what we resist will persist until we look at it
and accept it. If, rather than pushing our challenges
away, we can say to them, "I will not let you go unless
you bless me," we have taken a big step toward obtain-
ing that blessing. We look at our struggles "until the
breaking of the day," until we bring that which is hidden in the subconscious into the light of awareness.
Then the blessing takes place.

Striving With God

After Jacob said, "I will not let you go, unless you
bless me," the man gave him a new name. In the Bible,
a name change is very significant. In this context, a
person's name describes his or her nature or state of
consciousness. Jacob had a change of consciousness,
a spiritual awakening. This was the gift within the problem. The name *Israel* was given not only to Jacob, but
also to the nation of his descendants. *Israel* means "He
who strives with God."

One meaning of the word *strive* is "to make great
effort." Ironically, it takes great effort to overcome resistance. This effort, however, is not the effort of personal will, born out of fear and stubbornness; rather,
it is the deliberate effort to overcome our habits of unawareness and resistance. To "strive with God" can
mean to make great effort and know that God is our
ally; it can mean to strive with God as our partner.

Striving in this way leads to spiritual awakening. Striving out of personal willfulness simply creates more resistance and more suffering. Striving out of personal will alone is striving against God, and the result is suffering. To "strive with God" is to overcome the deeply ingrained habit of the personal will needing to be in control, needing to have the answers, needing to feel safe and secure. To strive with God is to be willing to be vulnerable, to live in trust, to accept God's will in our lives.

We are spiritual beings having human experiences. Our work is to discover ourselves as spiritual and human at the same time. Our humanness is an expression of our spirituality. We can know this intellectually—that is a good start—but it is not enough. We must bring the knowledge of our spiritual nature right into the core of our human awareness. One way we do this is through daily prayer and meditation. Another way is to practice the Truth we know in our everyday life experiences.

In our experiences of suffering, we are called on to struggle, to search, to surrender in ways we would not consider if we were not given this assignment. When life is unfolding comfortably and according to our expectations, we may have less incentive to search with the same zeal as when we are motivated by suffering. The experience of dis-ease is an opportunity to awaken. It is an opportunity to come into a deeper and fuller realization of who and what we really are.

Through the practice of nonresistance and holding the vision of a gift within the problem, we turn appar-

ent stumbling blocks into stepping-stones for transformation. By not resisting our crucifixions, we open the
door for our resurrections. By being willing to struggle
with ourselves and to strive with God as our ally, we
open the door to a change of consciousness. This is
rarely an easy process, but it is always a meaningful
one. The spiritual pearls of wisdom, love, power, and
freedom lie waiting for us through and beyond the appearance of disease and the experience of suffering.

A Story of Healing

Dr. Rachel Naomi Remen tells of a patient with bone
cancer:

> His leg was removed at the hip to save his
> life. He was twenty-four years old when I
> started working with him and he was a very
> angry man with a lot of bitterness. He felt a
> deep sense of injustice and a very deep hatred
> for all well people, because it seemed so un-
> fair to him that he had suffered this terrible
> loss so early in life.
>
> I worked with this man through his grief
> and rage and pain using painting, imagery,
> and deep psychotherapy. After working with
> him for more than two years there came a
> profound shift. He began "coming out of him-
> self." Later he started to visit other people who
> had suffered severe physical losses and he

would tell me the most wonderful stories about these visits.

Once he visited a young woman who was almost his own age. It was a hot day in Palo Alto and he was in running shorts so his artificial leg showed when he came into her hospital room. The woman was so depressed about the loss of both her breasts that she wouldn't even look at him, wouldn't pay attention to him. The nurses had left her radio playing, probably in order to cheer her up. So, desperate to get her attention, he unstrapped his leg and began dancing around the room on one leg, snapping his fingers to the music. She looked at him in amazement, and then burst out laughing and said, "Man, if you can dance, I can sing."

It was a year following this that we sat down to review our work together. He talked about what was significant to him and then I shared what was significant in our process. As we were reviewing our two years of work together, I opened his file and there discovered several drawings he had made early on. I handed them to him. He looked at them and said, "Oh, look at this." He showed me one of his earliest drawings. I had suggested that he draw a picture of his body. He had drawn a picture of a vase, and running through the vase was a deep, black crack. This was the image of his body and he had taken a black crayon and had drawn the crack over and over again. He was grinding his teeth with rage at the time. It was very, very painful because it seemed to him that this vase could never function as a vase again. It could never hold water.

Now, several years later, he came to this picture and looked at it and said "Oh, this one isn't finished." And I said, extending the box of crayons, "Why don't you finish it?" He picked a yellow crayon and putting his finger on the crack he said, "You see, here—where it is broken—this is where the light comes through." And with the yellow crayon he drew light streaming through the crack in his body.[15]

Mile Markers

- Spiritual healing begins when we recognize the need for our own healing of consciousness and then turn to God for help.

- Spiritual healing requires that we take responsibility for our part in the healing process. God always works through us, not for us.

- We open the door for healing when we see our suffering as a stepping-stone rather than as a stumbling block.

- An attitude of nonresistance toward our condition opens us to seeing the "gift within the problem."

- If we pay attention with an open mind and an open heart, resurrection will always follow a crucifixion.

- Rather than trying to rid ourselves of a condition of suffering, it is wiser to say, "I will not let you go, unless you bless me."

- A condition of dis-ease is both the cause and the result of struggling with ourselves. When we "strive with God," we are engaging God as an ally in our journey of healing.

Chapter Four Notes

1. Richard Bach, *Illusions* (New York: Dell, 1979), p. 71.
2. Carl Jung as quoted in Dick B., *The Akron Genesis of Alcoholics Anonymous* (Corte Madera, California: Good Book Publishing, 1992), p. 327. See also *Pass It On* (New York: Alcoholics Anonymous World Services, Inc., 1984), p. 384.
3. Jean Houston, *The Search for the Beloved* (Los Angeles: Jeremy P. Tarcher, Inc., 1987), p. 106.
4. Kat Duff as quoted in Gregg Levoy, *Callings* (New York: Three Rivers Press, 1998), p. 97.
5. Rachel Naomi Remen, M.D., *Kitchen Table Wisdom* (New York: Riverhead Books, 1997), p. 88–9.
6. Ibid., p.89.
7. Imelda Octavia Shanklin, *What Are You?* (Unity Village, Missouri: Unity Books, 1995), p. 146.
8. Ram Dass, *Still Here* (New York: Riverhead Books, 2000), p. 5.
9. Andrea Nelson, "Chaos Theory and Depression," as quoted in John E. Nelson and Andrea Nelson, *Sacred Sorrows* (New York: Jeremy P. Tarcher/Putnam, 1996), p. 133.
10. Ibid., pp. 134–5.
11. Levoy, p. 87.
12. Bach, p. 177.
13. Maulana Jalal al-Din Rumi, *The Essential Rumi*, translated by Coleman Barks (New York: HarperSanFrancisco, 1996), p. 109.

14. Marilyn Ferguson, *The Aquarian Conspiracy* (Los Angeles: J. P. Tarcher, Inc., 1980), p. 76.
15. Rachel Naomi Remen as quoted in *Soul Food*, edited by Jack Kornfield and Christina Feldman (New York: HarperSanFrancisco, 1996), pp. 28–9.

Adventure Four

Spiritual Alchemy: The Transformation of Suffering

When the crucifixion comes and you are suffering the pangs of dying error, you may cry out, "My God, my God, why hast thou forsaken me?" forgetting for the time the promises in the mount of Transfiguration. This is when you need to realize that you are passing through a transforming process that will be followed by a resurrection of all that is worth saving.

—Charles Fillmore[1]

How are you responding to your present life experiences? Typically we are happy with those experiences that feel good and conform with our expectations of how things "should" be. Conversely, we are usually unhappy with those experiences that are uncomfortable and do not fulfill our desires and expectations.

See if you can begin responding to each life experi-

---

[1] Charles Fillmore, *Atom-Smashing Power of Mind* (Unity Village, Missouri: Unity Books, 1995), p. 155.

ence with greater equanimity, that is, accepting each experience with nonresistance, with a balanced mind and heart. Don't wait for a calamity before you start practicing nonresistance. Begin with the small challenges in your life. If you do experience a major crucifixion, you can meet it with nonresistance because you will already have a firm foundation to build upon. This foundation is the ground from which the resurrection emerges.

Soul-Talk

I accept the gift that lies within every challenge in my life.

Write this declaration three times, pausing between each line to allow the statement to saturate your consciousness. Then say it aloud or silently as often as possible each day.

1. _____

2. _____

3. _____

Soul-Thoughts

 After you have completed writing your Soul-Talk, take time to sit quietly and observe your thoughts and feelings. Write them down.

As you consider a particular condition of suffering that you may be experiencing, explore your attitude toward this condition by answering the following questions. Answer them as honestly as you can.

 1. Am I recognizing the need for my own healing of consciousness?

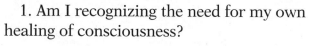 2. Am I willing to be changed? What might be my resistance to being changed?

3. Am I willing to turn to God for help and to surrender to God's direction for my life?

4. How am I responding to this condition?

5. Am I taking responsibility for my response to the condition? What are other possible responses?

6. Am I willing to take responsibility for my part in the healing process? What do I see as my responsibility in this process?

7. Am I open to the possibility of a blessing, a gift, a "pearl" within this challenge? If not, how might I open my awareness to that possibility?

Off the Main Trail

Describe your relationship to a condition of suffering. Describe the relationship as if it were a relationship with another person. What do you have to say to this condition? What does it have to say to you? Dialogue with the condition as you would dialogue with a person.

Stepping-Stone

 Practice observing your responses to all the experiences in your life. Practice this every day. Don't try to change anything— just notice. Don't analyze or judge yourself— just observe your responses to the various experiences in your daily life. Record your observations.

I accept the gift that lies within
every challenge in my life.

Chapter Five

Responsibility:
The Double-Edged Sword

> God gives Himself to man, and man has
> the power to make himself what he will.
> Freedom of will is man's inheritance, and
> he can use that freedom to build or destroy
> as he determines.
> —Charles Fillmore[1]

We now explore a very important principle—one
that is essential in the quest for wholeness. This is the
principle of responsibility. When used with wisdom, it
is an effective ally in our journey toward wholeness.
Using the principle of responsibility wisely can be the
key to healing and transformation. When used unwisely,
without right understanding, it can cause great suffering and delay our progress.

The journey to wholeness begins when we are willing to take responsibility for our part in the healing
process. To do this, we must first understand what
responsibility is, and what our part is in the healing
process. Without this understanding we may create un-
necessary suffering and we may delay our healing.

One error that we can make is to take too little responsibility for our part in the healing process. Our

culture usually sees an illness as something that happens *to* us. From this viewpoint, the sufferer must turn to some external agent—such as medicine, surgery, or divine intervention—as a cure for his or her suffering. This view sees the patient as having little responsibility in the process except for following the directions of the healer. Within this framework we can take a rather passive role. Here we see both the cause and the cure originating outside of us.

This traditional view sees the sufferer as a victim of some external agent; for example, a virus, old age, heredity, or bad luck. In contrast, it sees the healer as the wielder of some arcane magic that intervenes and saves the sufferer from his or her plight. The magic may be that of modern medical science or that of some supernatural healing power. In either case, it sees the magic lying in the hands of the healer, not the patient. It sees that healing is the special talent of a select group of people who are primarily responsible for the healing process. The patient is responsible only for following the directions of the expert.

By contrast, a metaphysical[2] paradigm sees the origin of all disease to be in the mind. In this view, all of the external circumstances of our lives are reflections of our beliefs, thoughts, and emotions. This view sees a person's life as a reflection of his or her consciousness. If held in mind, a false belief or negative emotion will eventually manifest itself as a malady in one's life. This malady can appear as physical illness, emotional disorder, relationship difficulties, financial problems, or any variety of challenges. This system sees healing not in the application of an external agent, but in the change of one's beliefs and attitudes. This framework puts the responsibility for both the problem and the healing squarely on the person experiencing the challenge.

The Double-Edged Sword

The idea that each individual is responsible for his or her life experience is like a double-edged sword—it can cut in two directions. On the one edge, it cuts through the belief that we are victims of blind chance or happenstance. It empowers the individual to be in charge of his or her own life and life experience. It shows the individual that the cause and the cure lie within, not without. This enables us to see no disease or condition as incurable for the cause and the cure lie within ourselves—within our own minds. In this view, we are all in control of our own thoughts and beliefs and therefore we are all responsible for our own suffering and our own healing.

Now let's look at the other edge. This edge of the sword can cut in a way that does not empower us or serve our well-being. It can create much suffering and inhibit genuine healing. Let us clearly recognize that this second edge of the sword is not an inherent part of a metaphysical belief system. It is the result of an error in perception. This error in perception originates in our conditioned tendency to judge everything as good or bad.

Our human inclination is to see that which is pleasant

and agreeable with our personal desires as good; conversely, we tend to see that which is unpleasant and that which thwarts our desires as bad. Illness is not pleasant and is rather inconvenient; therefore, we judge it to be bad. We usually see financial problems, emotional upsets, relationship difficulties as bad because they also are unpleasant and inconvenient. We usually label anything that is painful or difficult as "bad."[3]

This pronouncement of goodness and badness is erroneous. Pain is pain. Pleasure is pleasure. Getting what you want is getting what you want, and not getting what you want is not getting what you want. None of it is good or bad—it just is what it is. Our judgments are the only source of all goodness and badness, not the experience itself. The concept of good and bad exists only within the human mind; it has no inherent reality whatever.

If I believe that I create my own suffering through my thoughts and beliefs and if I see suffering as bad, then it follows that if I am suffering, I must be bad—or at best, ignorant or inept. The same mind-set that judges suffering as bad judges *me* as bad because I believe that I have caused the suffering. We can then view human suffering as evidence of a sin one has committed: the sin being that of harboring false beliefs or negative feelings, which are considered bad because they cause bad things to happen. This perception then creates a sense of guilt or shame within the sufferer. This is the edge of the sword where we can hurt ourselves if we are not careful. Rather than simply acknowledging responsibility, we take on guilt or shame.

Guilt is the feeling that we did something bad. Shame is the feeling that we *are* bad. Guilt is rarely helpful.[4] Shame never is. Shame never contributes to healing and always causes more suffering. Shame results from the belief that we are flawed and that we must hide our defectiveness. This sense of shame can cause people to isolate themselves from others at the very time they most need the love and support of other people. When we are suffering—be it physically, mentally, or emotionally—we need love and support from those around us. Historically, one reason human beings form community is to provide support for those who are suffering and need help. We have long recognized that we need one another, especially in times of crisis. To isolate ourselves in times of suffering may be to refuse the very help that supports our healing.

The sense of shame that can arise from these perceptions may be even more intense than it is in a religion which sees us as sinners bound for hell in a handbasket. In that system, *everyone* is a sinner. I can at least rationalize that I am "no worse than anyone else." However, in this second-edge of the sword scenario, I may feel an extraordinary amount of shame because I am "uniquely bad or inept." I may say to myself such things as these: "Not everyone gets cancer"; "Not everyone goes bankrupt"; "Not everyone gets divorced (or at least not as often as I do)."

To make matters worse, when my healing does not seem to occur, I can feel an even greater burden of guilt. The implication is that "not only did I cause this situation through my own ignorance or ineptitude, but I can't even heal it using principles I espouse to be true." We then pile frustration on top of the guilt.

This attitude of judgment may not only be in the mind of the sufferer but may also be in the mind of his or her companions: "What is it in his consciousness that drew that illness (or whatever) to him?" "If he were practicing his Truth principles, he would have healed that condition." (Even if this judgment is not taking place, the sufferer often projects this judgment onto others.) This unspoken question exacerbates the guilt of the sufferer and it may prevent his or her companions from having compassion and true caring for someone who needs it. It also may feed a subtle pride in those who are not (visibly) suffering: "If he 'had it together' like me, he wouldn't have that problem!"

If there is an underlying sense of shame in having a problem, then it tempts people to suppress their own suffering in an attempt to "be okay." This suppression can lead to the manifestation of some major problems that could have been averted if they had tended to them sooner.

We repeat an earlier statement: This problem of judgment, guilt, and shame is not part of the metaphysical philosophy itself but is the result of our conditioned tendency to label almost everything as good or bad. We live in a culture that is fraught with shame and with an obsession for "looking good" to mitigate this shame. Any philosophy that holds a view radically different from that of the prevalent culture always risks the danger of being misinterpreted or misused. When one attempts to view this philosophy through the eyes of the prevalent culture, it can lead to serious misunderstanding. For example, the statement "There is no evil" is a basic premise of metaphysics. This appears ridiculous to one who interprets this statement from the common viewpoint, which considers appearances to be real. Yet this is a very profound statement when seen from the perspective of one who really understands it. It is the *contamination* of the metaphysical philosophy by our cultural judgments that is the cause of this misunderstanding and misuse.

Gautama Buddha recognized how any spiritual teaching is subject to misuse. One of the Buddha's sermons is named "The Simile of a Snake." It refers to the proper use and the misuse of spiritual teachings. He said that if a snake is grasped by the tail it may bite us, but if we grasp it by the back of the head we can handle it safely. He went on to say that any spiritual teaching is similar.[5] If used unwisely, it can "bite us"; that is, it can create suffering rather than healing. We must grasp every spiritual teaching "behind the head"; that is, we must use it as it was meant to be used. It must be understood as it was by the person who originated the teaching. Any spiritual teaching is subject to misunderstanding and misuse. The *misuse* of a spiritual teaching often *creates suffering* rather than healing.

Responsibility does not imply guilt. To acknowledge responsibility without guilt and blame is to acknowledge one's own power as a creative being. Wise responsibility empowers everyone concerned. Shame and guilt perpetuate the illusion of good and bad, right and wrong. Shame and guilt perpetuate the illusion that we are inherently bad and must redeem ourselves by appearing good or wise or competent. This is the antithesis of true responsibility, which sees each person empowered with the ability to shape his or her own life. By stepping out of guilt, shame, and blame, we step into true responsibility, which will empower us to become cocreators of our life experiences.

The Question of Cause

When we consider the principle of responsibility, many questions inevitably arise: Do we cause *all* of the circumstances in our lives? If so, why would we cause our own suffering? And what about infants and young children who have not yet developed cognitive abilities? How could they be responsible for their own suffering?

This issue of causality is very complex and perhaps paradoxical. First, we often see cases where an individual seems to have caused his or her own suffering by abusing the body or by behaving recklessly. Conversely, we often see cases where it seems there is no way the person caused his or her own suffering. Possible examples are these: an infant with a birth defect; a child grieving the death of a parent; a person whose house is demolished by a tornado.

Furthermore, when we think that we have identified

a cause for something, we can always ask the question "What caused the 'cause'?" We can repeat this endlessly, looking for an "ultimate cause": "The cause of my illness is suppressed anger." "The cause of my anger is childhood abuse." "The cause of my childhood abuse is that I was an abuser in a past life." "The cause of my being an abuser in a past life was that I was abused in the lifetime before that. . . ."

Finally, we can see that few things have singular causes. Virtually every event is the result of many factors: What causes it to rain? What caused the Civil War? What is the cause of cancer? These questions defy simplistic answers because they each have multiple causes that interrelate in complex ways.

Getting bogged down in endless speculation is not conducive to spiritual healing. This could be called "the paralysis of analysis." Historically, great spiritual teachers have refused to get caught in the entanglement of speculative questions. In the Gospel of John is the story of Jesus' disciples seeing a man blind from birth. They ask Jesus, "Rabbi, who sinned, this man or his parents, that he was born blind?" (This is the biblical equivalent of the question "What was it in his consciousness that caused his blindness?") Jesus responded, "It was not that this man sinned, or his parents, but that the works of God might be made manifest in him" (Jn. 9:2–3). Jesus refused to engage in some speculation of cause. He went right to the basic Truth that we are here to express God and that the conditions of our lives are exactly what we need to do that.

The Buddha's disciples pressed him for answers to

similar speculative questions. He responded with this parable:

> Suppose . . . a man were wounded by an arrow thickly smeared with poison, and his friends and companions, his kinsmen and relatives, brought a surgeon to treat him. The man would say: "I will not let the surgeon pull out this arrow until I know whether the man who wounded me was a noble or a brahmin or a merchant or a worker." And he would say: "I will not let the surgeon pull out this arrow until I know the name and clan of the man who wounded me; . . . until I know whether the man who wounded me was tall or short or of middle height; . . . until I know whether the man who wounded me was dark or brown or golden-skinned; . . . until I know whether the man who wounded me lives in such a village or town or city; . . . until I know whether the bow that wounded me was a longbow or a crossbow; . . . until I know whether the bowstring that wounded me was fibre or reed or sinew. . . ."
>
> All this would still not be known to that man and meanwhile he would die.[6]

For thousands of years humankind has been speculating on why things are as they are. Many philosophies and many theologies have attempted to give a final and authoritative answer to this question. Each one has answered some questions but raised many others in the process. Ultimately, we don't know. Perhaps words and ideas are not able to convey the ultimate nature of things. Maybe we should shift our question from "What caused this?" to "What am I to do with the life experience that I've been given?" Gregg Levoy writes:

> Rather than using sickness as an opportunity to beat yourself up, or set off on a crusade to figure out why bad things happen to good people, better to try and use illness and pain for what they were designed for—to get your attention. Understand that though you may not have created them, your soul may still be attempting to communicate something to you through them. We are not so much responsible *for* our illnesses, says author and Buddhist teacher Stephen Levine, as we are responsible *to* our illnesses. The question is not so much what to do *about* our suffering, but what to do *with* it.
>
> Being responsible *to* an illness, he says, means being willing to relate to it, have a full-on experience of it, and investigate not just the pain but also your reaction to it. It means letting it communicate with you rather than merely trying to subdue it.[7]

We can ask, "What did I do to cause my disease?" But it is much more helpful to ask, "What am I doing to be a cause for my healing?" When we honestly ask ourselves this question, we have taken a major step toward creating wholeness. We begin to be a cause for our own healing when we are willing to be responsible for that which is our true responsibility.

Our True Responsibility

What then is our responsibility? The root of the word *responsibility* is *response*. The root of our responsibility lies in our response to life. We are responsible for our response to any experience, event, or condition. Our response to any experience is based upon our perception of it. We are responsible for how we perceive each experience in our lives. Our perception of each experience determines the meaning that we give to it. We are responsible for the meaning that we give to each experience in our lives.

We are conditioned to believe that our response is an inevitable reaction to what is and that the meaning we give something is what it really means. Our cultural belief is that our perceptions are an accurate interpretation of some external reality. We often fail to see that we create the meaning of everything we experience through our interpretation of the experience. An old joke tells the story of a man who looks at a series of inkblots and sees nothing but sexual images each time. When the psychologist suggests that the man is obsessed with sex, he responds "Me? *You're* the one showing me all these obscene pictures!" We may do the same with the persons, events, and conditions in our lives.

We often experience something and then interpret its meaning as if the meaning were inherent in the experience itself rather than something that we give to it.

We give the meaning to everything we experience. The meaning that we give determines our response. Even if we were to believe that we had no power over the conditions of our lives, we would still have complete power over how we choose to respond to those conditions. No matter what the condition in our lives, we can respond to it any way that we choose.

Viktor Frankl, a Jewish psychiatrist, spent three terrible years in Nazi concentration camps. More than ninety-five percent of all prisoners died. Amidst very miserable conditions he discovered a basic Truth.

> We who lived in concentration camps can remember the men who walked through the huts comforting others, giving away their last piece of bread. They may have been few in number, but they offer sufficient proof that everything can be taken from a man but one thing: the last of the human freedoms—to choose one's attitude in any given set of circumstances, to choose one's own way.[8]

No set of conditions can determine our attitude. Only we can determine our attitude. This is our ultimate freedom and our ultimate power. We are deeply conditioned to believe that the conditions of our lives dictate our attitudes and our beliefs. The Truth is that we and we alone are in control of our beliefs and attitudes.

Wayne Muller, a minister and psychologist, tells of a friend:

> Four years ago Kirsten received a completely unexpected diagnosis: During a routine mammogram, it was discovered she had a tumor in her breast. It proved to be malignant. Even worse, cancer cells had invaded her lymph system. The prognosis was not hopeful.
>
> Kirsten instantly responded to this information in a variety of ways. She assembled a team of physicians and healers. She had the tumor removed and began a course of chemotherapy. She combined Western medicine with Chinese herbs, acupuncture, and other healing techniques. She addressed her illness with tremendous mindfulness and care.
>
> But Kirsten then rearranged other things in her life. She cut back on her work. Since she was making less money, she simplified her days. She stayed home more, took walks, and worked in her beloved vegetable garden. She had tea with people she loved. She did yoga, she meditated, she lay in her hammock and listened to breezes. She started to paint. The reality of her cancer focused Kirsten's awareness on the fundamental quality of her life. She had always wanted to deepen her spiritual practice, she had always wanted to gar-

den, she had always wanted to paint. If not now, when?

Happily, Kirsten lived to heal from her cancer. Her life is again more busy, but the fundamental flavor of her enjoyment of life lingers. "I am so grateful for my life," she said to me the other day over lunch. "I don't take anything for granted. Every day is a miracle. Before, I would just make it through the day, as if it was all just work. Now I feel such joy to just be alive each day. I am much happier, life is lighter. I only give my care and attention to what is really important—being loving, being kind, creating beauty, being grateful."[9]

Kirsten saw that she was responsible for how she responded to her condition. She responded by creating the life she had always desired in her heart. Would that we all do that before we are stricken with a life-threatening illness!

Often we respond to conflict or disease the same way we would respond to a problem with our automobile: "Let's get it fixed so that I can 'get on' with life." We see suffering as a problem to be solved. We see each problem as an impediment to our "real lives" and think that the problem should be solved as soon as possible. The remedy is sought with a problem-solving approach similar to the way we would diagnose a problem with our automobile engine: "What is it in my consciousness that needs fixing?"

Whether we use medication or herbs or affirmations, we may still be envisioning healing as a process of fixing something that is broken. We then continue our life journey with the same set of assumptions, beliefs, and opinions. True wholeness occurs only when we are willing to use our experience of suffering as an opportunity to reevaluate our deepest beliefs and, ultimately, our lives themselves. Transformation occurs only when we are willing to be changed deeply rather than simply putting a patch on our existing self-image and belief systems.

The reevaluation of our assumptions may help us see that healing could lie in *not* trying to fix ourselves and simply accepting "what is." A simple acceptance of what is sometimes provides the foundation for the very healing we so earnestly seek. Wayne Muller tells of a woman named Jacqueline who came to one of his retreats:

> She had been hurt deeply as a child by her abusive parents. They had harmed her physically and emotionally . . . .
>
> But Jacqueline had also done a great deal of work on herself. In therapy . . . she found within herself places of great strength and spiritual courage. She was ready to let go of her parents, she said; she had done forgiveness meditations, tried letting them go, tried saying good-bye to the past. Yet still, when she thought of them, she felt anger and hurt.

She was frustrated and disappointed in herself. Why hadn't she been able to finally let them go?

I suggested she stop trying to let them go. . . . "I get so impatient, I want this whole thing to be over," she replied. Her voice was tired, frustrated. "I just want to be finished with them."

"Perhaps it is merely this impatience that stops this process from moving forward," I suggested. "Maybe you could allow even this feeling of incompleteness to be enough for now. To simply rest in the readiness for it to happen, without pushing so hard all the time to make it happen."

Jacqueline seemed to relax. She smiled. "Actually," she admitted, "I wouldn't mind a little rest. . . ."

Two weeks later, Jacqueline sent me a letter. "You'll never believe this, . . . but I *did* stop pushing my parents to leave, and I just surrendered into waiting. And then, without me doing anything, one morning I woke up and I felt different. They were gone. My parents were completely gone. . . . They just fell away. It feels wonderful."[10]

Stephen Levine says that "acceptance is magic."[11] Genuine acceptance has a mysterious power that moves us in the direction of wholeness.

The Creator Game

We have seen earlier that trying to determine the cause of an event or condition can lead to endless, and fruitless, speculation. However, we can adopt an attitude about the causes of the events and conditions of our lives that may be tremendously empowering. Adopting this attitude is like playing a game. I call it the "creator game." We can choose to play this game, if we wish, simply because it may empower us to do so. The game is optional; no one is required to play. In fact, you *can't* play it if you believe that you are required to!

To play the creator game, we must be willing to drop another game if we are playing it. The game we must drop is the "right-wrong" game (also known as the "good-bad" game). We cannot play "right-wrong" and "creator" at the same time. The two are incompatible. To play the creator game, we must let go of all blame and judgment. We must let go of all notions of things being good or bad, right or wrong. In place of the judgment of good and bad, we simply see that some things make life work well and some things don't. Some things cause suffering and some things cause satisfaction. We term what works and causes satisfaction *skillful*. We call what doesn't work and causes suffering *unskillful*. In this game, neither one is better than the other. Neither one is good and neither one is bad.

Another game we must drop if we are to play the creator game is the "victim game." The victim game is similar to "right-wrong." This game always sees someone (usually me) as the victim of some great injustice perpetrated by him, her, them, or the Universe in general. "Ain't It Awful" is the theme song for players of the victim game. This, too, must go if we are to be creators.

To play the creator game, we assume that we are 100 percent responsible for everything we experience— both our reactions *and* the events and conditions themselves. We assume this responsibility simply because we choose to. Is it true? Who knows? This may be an unanswerable question. Perhaps the ultimate answer is "It's up to us whether or not it's true."

Once upon a time there lived a very wise sage. His home was (of course) a temple in the Himalayas. His wisdom was renowned. Tales of his great wisdom had spread throughout the land. It was even said that there was *no* question he could not answer correctly.

Upon hearing this, a very wily young lad from a nearby village requested an audience with the sage. He was granted his request and he stood before the sage. He held his hands behind his back and put forth his question: "O great sage, I am holding a bird behind me. Is this bird I am holding alive or dead?"

The bird was actually alive. If the sage responded "Dead," the lad would simply produce the living bird and prove him wrong. If the sage responded "Alive," the clever (and ruthless) lad would wring the bird's neck and produce a dead bird. The boy stood with a smug smile on his face, waiting for the sage to reply.

The wise man closed his eyes for several seconds.

Then a charitable smile appeared on his face. He opened his eyes and replied gleefully, "Son, the answer to that question lies in *your* hands."

Knowing that the answer lies in our hands, we can play our creator game. To do this, we simply assume that we have created everything we experience. We are the authors of our lives. Our work, then, is to pay attention to what we have created.

"Why would I create a disease for my experience?" you may ask. "Why would I create suffering for myself?" I don't know. Take a look. Listen. Let the experience itself answer the question for you. Don't be analytical but just continue to live with the assumption that you are the author of your life. Answers will come but, most likely, not in ways that you expect them.

The goal is not to "figure things out" but to truly become the author of your life. The way to become the author of your life is to assume that you *always have been*. Take a look at what you've created. If you can take responsibility for this, then you will gradually receive the power to consciously create the life you desire.

Once again, this game is not for everyone. If you choose not to play it, it's okay. It doesn't mean anything that you've chosen not to play it. If you do choose to play it, remember that you have created *all* of it—the satisfaction, the suffering, the joy, the sorrow, the whole catastrophe. Have fun!

Mile Markers

- The principle of responsibility is an important principle in our quest for wholeness. Used wisely, it is the key to healing and transformation. Used unwisely, it can cause great suffering.

- One error we can make is not to take responsibility for our part in the healing process. Another error is to misunderstand the true meaning of responsibility.

- A metaphysical paradigm sees the origin of disease to be in the mind. In this view, all the circumstances of our lives are a reflection of our beliefs, thoughts, and emotions.

- This view can empower us or cause suffering. It cuts through the belief that we are victims of chance. It empowers us to be in charge of our own life experiences.

- On the other hand, it can lead to feelings of guilt or shame. We reason: If I am creating my own suffering through my thoughts and feelings, then I must be bad, ignorant, or inept.

- Guilt is *not* an inherent part of a metaphysical belief system. Any spiritual teaching is subject to misunderstanding and misuse. This creates suffering rather than healing.

- We are responsible for our responses to experiences. Our responses are based upon our perceptions. We are responsible for the meaning that we give to each experience.

- We can adopt an attitude about the events of our lives that can be very empowering. This is the "creator game." We can choose to believe that we are the authors of our life experiences.

Chapter Five Notes

1. Charles Fillmore, *Keep a True Lent* (Unity Village, Missouri: Unity Books, 1997), p. 29.
2. The term is used here to describe a specific form of metaphysics that views Divine Mind as the ultimate reality and humankind as cocreators of personal reality. This is the traditional view held by Unity and the New Thought movement in general. The term *metaphysics* can also be used more generally to identify *any* philosophy that inquires into the ultimate nature of reality.
3. We may not consciously use the word *bad,* but our emotional response is based on the perception that "this is bad."
4. Guilt can conceivably be helpful if it leads us to taking responsibility for our actions, seeking forgiveness from those we've harmed, and making amends, if necessary.
5. Gautama Buddha, "Alagaddūpama Sutta" in *The Middle Length Discourses of the Buddha: A New Translation of the Majjhima Nikāya* (Boston: Wisdom Publications, 1995), p. 227.
6. Ibid., "Cūlamālunkya Sutta," pp. 534–5.
7. Gregg Levoy, *Callings* (New York: Three Rivers Press, 1998), p. 91.
8. Viktor E. Frankl, *Man's Search for Meaning* (New York: Pocket Books, 1963), p. 104.

9. Wayne Muller, *How, Then, Shall We Live?* (New York: Bantam Books, 1997), pp. 154–5.
10. Ibid., pp. 185–6.
11. Stephen Levine, *Who Dies?* (New York: Anchor Press, 1982), p. 190.

Adventure Five

Responsibility:
The Double-Edged Sword

Everything we do or fail to do conditions its
own response. What we send out tends to come
back to us, increased and multiplied, like an echo.
Action calls for reaction. Cause and effect are root
and branch of the same tree.
　　　　　　　　　　　　　—Ernest C. Wilson[1]

When I was a child, being "responsible" meant feeling burdened, controlled, or "being watched." As an adult, I realize that none of this is inherent with responsibility. To understand the true meaning of responsibility, we may need to let go of some old ideas.

We can believe, think, say, and do whatever we choose. Responsibility is recognizing that we experience consequences for whatever we believe, think, say, and do. These consequences are not rewards for being good or punishments for being bad. Consequences are simply the natural results of our beliefs, thoughts, words, and actions.

---

[1] Ernest C. Wilson, *Like a Miracle* (Unity Village, Missouri: Unity Books, 1971), p. 21.

We begin practicing true responsibility when we acknowledge our responsibility for how we interpret and give meaning to each experience in our lives. Our responses to life are based upon these interpretations and meanings. Our future life experiences are conditioned by our responses to each experience in the present moment. Moment by moment we build our futures from the present.

Soul-Talk

I am the cocreator of my life experience.
Write this declaration three times, pausing between each line to allow the statement to saturate your consciousness. Then say it aloud or silently as often as possible each day.

1. _____

2. _____

3. _____

Soul-Thoughts

After you have completed writing your Soul-Talk, take time to sit quietly and observe your thoughts and feelings. Write them down.

Note: Please answer the following questions from the feeling level rather than the
rational level of mind.

1. List some personal life experiences that
you feel responsible for creating.

2. In what way do you feel that you created
these experiences?

3. For each of these experiences, do you
have any pride, guilt, or shame connected
with this sense of responsibility? Why?

4. List some personal life experiences that you do not feel responsible for creating.

5. How do you feel about these experiences? What does it mean to you that you have had these experiences?

6. Do you feel responsible for the meaning or interpretation you have of these experiences? Why or why not?

Off the Main Trail

 What is your immediate reaction to these words: You are responsible for your life experience. Explore that reaction. What emotions, memories, images come into your awareness? Write about this.

Stepping-Stone

As you experience the events of your everyday life, pay attention to your perception of these events. Which events do you feel responsible for? Do you feel responsible for your responses to these events? Do you feel responsible for the meaning that you give to these events? Keep a journal.

I am the cocreator of my life experience.

Chapter Six

Faith:
The Mind of Wholeness

> Faith is the inner assurance that what we
> desire already exists in the invisible realm of
> Spirit and can, by the *exercise* of our faith,
> be brought into being.
> —Elizabeth Sand Turner[1]

Faith and spiritual healing seem like natural partners. Some people regard all spiritual healing as "faith healing." Perhaps this particular term conjures up images of an old-fashioned tent revival: a Spirit-filled and sweat-soaked evangelist performs the "laying on of hands" for some afflicted soul kneeling before him. The two are surrounded by a frenzied crowd of believers who are singing, shaking, and swooning.

This scene portrays one form of faith healing, and it may be an effective form for some. We will, however, consider the term *faith* and its relationship to healing in a vastly broader context. We will not limit the form in which faith can work, nor will we limit the form through which healing can occur. And we do not put any limitation on what we mean by *healing*. Healing is open-ended and limitless in magnitude and form.

What Is Faith?

Faith, like wholeness itself, is a divine idea. A divine idea exists beyond the domain of time and space. We cannot describe it, define it, or conceptualize it. A divine idea has infinite possibilities for expressing itself within the realm of time and space. As with any divine idea, we can know faith only through direct experience. It is like the wind; we can see its effect but we cannot see the thing itself.

Faith can be expressed as a so-called miracle, and faith can be expressed in the quiet workings of nature. Its true character is a mystery. Its manifestations may be mysterious or commonplace. Faith is the power to see a possibility, and it is the power to realize that possibility.

Faith is the power to make the possible real. The object of our faith becomes real for us. Our very sense of reality depends on faith. It is the power that realizes (that is, makes real) images held in the mind.

Faith is intrinsic within the mind of every human being. It operates within each of us. We are often admonished to "have faith," but actually we cannot *not* have faith! Faith is fundamental to our nature. To have faith usually means to focus our faith in a particular direction. Yet faith is always operating in our consciousness, no matter how doubtful or fearful we may feel.

Fear is faith turned inside out. Fear is having faith in certain images created by the mind rather than having faith in the creative power of the mind itself. Our fearsome mental images may have their origin in prior personal experiences, or they may be the result of cultural conditioning. These memories may be filled with strong emotions. If we do not discharge this emotional energy from the body, these images will continue to haunt the mind. As we put our faith in these images, we make our fear real and thus we give it power over us. (The word *fear* can be used as an acronym for *f*alse *e*vidence *a*ppearing *r*eal.) A story from the East tells of an artist who painted a large picture of a tiger on the wall of his house. He was a very good artist and the picture appeared so real that he became afraid to enter his own house! So we too may frighten ourselves with our own imaginings when we imbue them with reality.

In a sense, we choose our reality because we, knowingly or unknowingly, choose where we place our faith. Very early in life we develop the perceptions that create our sense of reality. The choice of where we place our faith soon becomes habitual and unconscious. By the time we become adults, these habituated perceptions are deeply entrenched in the subconscious.

What we perceive to be reality is the result of several factors. One of these factors is our human physiology. Our physical characteristics are largely the result of our biological evolution. The physical characteristics of our sense organs and brain cause us to perceive the external world as it appears to us.

According to Carl Jung, we also have certain innate mental characteristics that affect our perception of reality. He called these characteristics *archetypes*. These archetypes influence the way we perceive and interpret the experiences of our lives. Which particular archetypes may influence us and how they influence us are the results of many factors. Our stage of life is one factor. Our culture and our particular era of human history are also factors in determining our perception of reality.

We also know that our personal histories affect our perceptions of reality. The characteristics of our families of origin strongly impact the way we see ourselves and our world. Certain life experiences—especially if intense or traumatic—may also impact the way we see certain people or circumstances.

Faith is the power to create our reality by our perceptions, our beliefs, and our interpretations.

Seeing is believing, and yet believing is seeing. According to our faith, our world reveals itself to us and becomes real.

Faith and Medical Science

Modern medicine has an ambiguous relationship with the concept of faith. Our modern allopathic system of medicine is grounded in the assumption of an objective natural reality functioning independently of our belief systems. In this view, medicine and surgery work simply because they change an objective reality. Yet every health professional knows that a patient's beliefs and emotions can have a major impact on his or her own healing process.

For many years physicians have known about the so-called placebo effect. They give a sugar pill or an injection of water to a patient but tell the patient that it is real medicine. Often this placebo works as effectively as the medicine itself. There have even been cases of placebo surgeries, where the patient has been cut open and then sewn back up with no surgical procedure taking place. Yet the patient has responded positively, as if he or she has undergone the full surgical procedure![2] These are forms of faith healing and they display the very tangible impact that one's beliefs can have on the physical body.

We will give a seemingly incredible example of the power of the placebo in a case reported by psychologist Bruno Klopfer. He was treating a man named Wright who was in the advanced stages of lymphatic cancer. His body was filled with tumors the size of oranges. His physician had exhausted all standard treatment and it appeared that death was inevitable. However, Wright had heard of a new drug named Krebiozen and he repeatedly begged his doctor to let him try it. At this stage of the disease, the doctor did not expect the drug to help but gave it to him simply to placate the patient's relentless demands.

Three days later Wright was up and walking around. He reported that his tumors had "melted like snowballs on a hot stove" and were half their original size. Ten days later Wright left the hospital, apparently cancer-free. When he had entered the hospital, he had needed an oxygen mask to breathe, but when he left, he was well enough to fly his own airplane at 12,000 feet with no discomfort.

He remained well for several weeks but then he heard about research indicating that Krebiozen had no effect on curing his form of cancer. Wright became very depressed, suffered a relapse, and was readmitted to the hospital. Then his physician decided to try an experiment. He told Wright that he had a new, improved version of Krebiozen that was highly effective. This was not so. He simply injected him with plain water.

Again, the results were dramatic. The tumor masses melted and Wright was quickly back on his feet. He remained symptom-free for several more weeks until the American Medical Association publicly announced that Krebiozen was worthless in the treatment of cancer. After he heard this, Wright's cancer symptoms returned, and he died two days later![3]

Can we say that all drugs are simply placebos? Is faith the only factor in the effectiveness of medicine? According to conventional medical science, the answer is clearly "no." A standard test to measure the efficacy of any new drug is to measure its results compared with a placebo. Clearly, many drugs seem to work despite the personal belief system of the patient. Not all healing seems to require the patient to have faith in the doctor or the medicine. Since medicine can heal without faith and faith can heal without medicine, it would appear that these two healing modalities are totally separate. This is the conventional viewpoint.

Perhaps this viewpoint is not correct, however. Perhaps the objective world of nature and the subjective world of faith are not separate at all, but are simply two facets of the same underlying reality. It could be that reality has an inner and an outer dimension and that healing can be effected from either one or both. Perhaps the body and mind are not separate at all but are simply the visible and invisible forms of a deeper reality. If this were true, then we would see nothing mysterious about healing accomplished by faith, by medical science, or by a placebo.

Besides the well-known placebo effect, many physicians have long been aware of the power of faith in healing but have been reluctant to publicly acknowledge this fact. Fortunately, this is changing. At the 1996 meeting of the American Academy of Family Physicians, ninety-nine percent of doctors surveyed said that religious beliefs can contribute to healing. Sixty-three percent of doctors said God had intervened to improve their own medical conditions.[4]

Research studies seem to confirm the doctors' belief in the power of faith to heal. As reported in the *Reader's Digest,* "A survey of 5,286 Californians found that church members have lower death rates than nonmembers—despite risk factors such as smoking, drinking, obesity, and inactivity. Those with a religious commitment had fewer symptoms or had better health outcomes in seven out of eight cancer studies, four out of five blood-pressure studies, four out of six heart-disease studies and four out of five general-health studies."[5]

One does not have to be a church member to have faith. Yet this study presumes that those who are church members have a greater degree of faith in a Higher Power than those who are not. Other factors, such as the effect of being part of a community, could also play a role in the higher degree of health among church members. Yet, at the very least, this study suggests that faith is a powerful element in both the healing and the prevention of disease.

I have a personal example of the power of faith to heal. In 1981 I was the minister of a Unity church in Indiana. Ordained in 1980, I was a "rookie," having had only six months on the job. Given the relatively frequent occurrence of cancer in our population, it did not surprise me that someone would come to me with a recent cancer diagnosis. What did surprise me was that this person was my wife!

Gayle walked into my office with tears in her eyes. She had just returned from her doctor's office. A few days earlier she had discovered three tumors in her breast. The doctor informed her that the tumors were malignant and were growing rapidly, and he encouraged her to have surgery very soon. Gayle was angry and frightened. She questioned her faith in Truth principles and her faith in God. Yet, beyond her fear, Gayle knew that healing was possible. She had read the story of Myrtle Fillmore's healing many times. "If it can happen to Myrtle, it can happen to me," she repeated to herself. We prayed and we talked (and we cried) many times. I asked her, "Which is more real,

God or the cancer?" Her faith said "God"; her fear said
"the cancer." She struggled. We both struggled with
our faith and our fear, our belief and our doubt.

The night before her scheduled surgery, Gayle couldn't
sleep. Frustrated, she went into the living room to meditate. Suddenly the room seemed filled with light and
she heard a voice: "Do you believe?" "Yes," she responded.
"Do you believe?" the voice repeated. "Yes." A third time,
"Do you believe?" "Yes!" she said angrily. Then something inside her snapped. She began to cry and she
said quietly, "Help my unbelief."

The light in the room disappeared and seemed to
appear inside her. She felt a great wave of peace and
knew that she had been healed. She went to bed and
slept peacefully.

When Gayle awoke the next morning, the tumors
had disappeared. She talked her reluctant physician
into giving her another exam before the surgery. He
did. He was amazed. The tumors were gone.

Gayle's experience may be typical of the spontaneous
healing process: an initial response of anger and fear;
a struggle between belief and doubt; a deepening of
faith through prayer; the final release of "unbelief"
followed by surrender and peace; the inner knowing
that healing has taken place; and then the physical evidence to show it.

Deepak Chopra writes:

> Research on spontaneous cures of cancer,
> conducted in both the United States and

Japan, has shown that just before the cure appears, almost every patient experiences a dramatic shift in awareness. He knows that he will be healed, and he feels that the force responsible is inside himself but not limited to him—it extends beyond his personal boundaries, throughout all of nature. Suddenly he feels, "I am not limited to my body. All that exists around me is part of myself." At that moment, such patients apparently jump to a new level of consciousness that prohibits the existence of cancer. Then the cancer cells either disappear, literally overnight in some cases, or at the very least stabilize without damaging the body any further.[6]

Let's examine this statement in greater detail because it explains some crucial elements within the spiritual healing process: "Just before the cure appears, almost every patient experiences a dramatic shift in awareness. He knows that he will be healed. . . ."

Usually, the knowing precedes the physical experience. We refer to this knowing as faith. Faith knows something to be real before the physical appearance of that reality. This faith is the result of "a dramatic shift in awareness." This shift in awareness is the reversal of our ordinary awareness, which believes that "only when I see it, is it real."

How does this shift occur? Can we will it? Why does it occur for some and not for others?

We cannot directly will this shift into faith, but we must be willing to *let* it happen. This shift can begin with a conscious desire for more faith, and perhaps it must begin with a desire for faith. Yet the experience of faith seems to come only *after* we surrender. At first we see faith as something to get but then our attitude shifts to one of allowing faith to enter: "He feels that the force responsible is inside himself but not limited to him—it extends beyond his personal boundaries, throughout all of nature."

When we experience faith, it seems that it is a connection to something much greater than the personal self and yet it is not entirely outside us. Faith is both the cause and the result of this connection. Faith occurs when we know that we are not separate, isolated beings but an integral part of a much greater wholeness. This wholeness is not only our own essential nature but it is the essential nature of the universe: "Suddenly he feels, I am not limited to my body. All that exists around me is part of myself."

The notion of our oneness with all that exists is found in all mystical literature. The idea that our separate existence is an illusion is the foundation of the Western mystical tradition and of most Eastern philosophies. It is a corollary to Unity's foundation principle, which states, "There is only one Presence and one Power in the universe."

A second major premise of Unity's teaching is that we create our experiences with our thoughts and beliefs. Eastern teachings say much the same. The Buddha said: "We are what we think. All that we are arises with our thoughts. With our thoughts we make the world."[7]

Faith and Physics

What is most fascinating is that the science of quantum physics may be telling us the same thing. Quantum physics has turned upside down the basic premise of Newtonian science, which is that reality exists outside us and that we are independent observers of a pre-existing independent reality. Fred Alan Wolf writes:

> What do we mean when we speak of "reality"? We usually mean the world that we sense. The world out there is made up of things that we can see, hear, taste, smell, and touch— real, solid, substantial objects of our everyday existence. We take it for granted that these things would exist in their same sensible form even if we were not there to observe them. Our observations simply verify an already existing reality.
>
> Yet, that isn't what quantum mechanics seems to be telling us. It appears to indicate a drastic departure from what we could call our classical mechanical heritage. Certainly this is the position of what later came to be

known as the Copenhagen School or the Bohr Principle of Complementarity. According to the tenets of the complementarity principle, there is no reality until that reality is perceived. . . .

The reason for this paradoxical appearance of reality—at least, atomic reality as observed by physicists— is that no clear dividing line exists between ourselves and the reality we observe to exist outside of ourselves. Instead, reality depends upon our choices of what and how we choose to observe. These choices, in turn, depend upon our minds or, more specifically, the content of our thoughts.[8]

In a sense, Wolf is speaking of faith when he says, "Reality depends upon our choices of what and how we choose to observe." He echoes our statement that faith is the power which creates our reality. Our belief that reality exists outside ourselves is the result of "our choices of what and how we choose to observe." It would be just as valid to assume that the world we see outside of us is as much a part of us as our own thoughts and feelings.

I once heard a Native American medicine man telling about a tribal rain dance in which he participated. A white male in the audience asked him how he could possibly believe that his dancing and chanting could affect the weather. The medicine man responded by

asking the questioner to move his finger. He did. Then
the medicine man asked, "How is it that you can move
your finger?" The man frowned and said, "I can move
my finger because it's part of me." The medicine man
responded: "Exactly. And when you see all of nature as
part of you, then you will see that what you do can
affect the weather."

The Native American rain dance can be seen as an
act of faith—not simply a faith in supplications to an
omnipotent God, but also a faith based on knowledge
of the oneness of all life. The faith which heals, the
faith which moves us into wholeness, is this faith
which is grounded in the reality of the oneness of all
life.

Faith, Science, and the Bible

The biblical writer of The Letter to the Hebrews
tells us that faith is "the assurance of things hoped for,
the conviction of things not seen" (Heb. 11:1). Faith is
the certainty, the conviction, that an ultimate Reality
lies beyond the apparent reality of the external universe. The same writer goes on to say, "By faith we understand that the world was created by the word of
God, so that what is seen was made out of things
which do not appear" (Heb. 11:3). Interestingly, some
scientists may be agreeing with this biblical statement.

Physicist David Bohm has postulated the existence
of an *implicate,* or *enfolded order,* that is the invisible
source of the visible world which we inhabit. He calls
our visible world of time and space the *explicate,* or

unfolded order. Bohm sees our world—the explicate order—as having been created much in the way a holographic image is created, and this image is a projection of a deeper reality—the implicate order. Marilyn Ferguson says:

> What appears to be a stable, tangible, visible, audible world, said Bohm, is an illusion. It is dynamic and kaleidoscopic—not really "there." What we normally see is the explicit, or unfolded, order of things, rather like watching a movie. But there is an underlying order that is mother and father to this second-generation reality. He called the other order implicate, or enfolded. The enfolded order harbors our reality, much as the DNA in the nucleus of the cell harbors potential life and directs the nature of its unfolding.[9]

If the visible world is but a hologram, why does it appear so real to us? The answer to this question may be found in the work of Karl Pribram, a neuroscientist, who says, "Maybe reality isn't what we see with our eyes."[10] Ferguson explains: "Our brains mathematically construct 'hard' reality by interpreting frequencies from a dimension transcending time and space. The brain is a hologram, interpreting a holographic universe."[11]

The writer of Hebrews tells us that the world was created by "the word of God." What is this "word of God" that has the power to create the visible from the

invisible? It is the creative power of faith called forth
into expression. Charles Fillmore defines *faith* as "the
perceiving power of the mind linked with a power to
shape substance."[12] Through the power of faith, we
perceive that which is real and we bring it forth into
expression in our world.

Faith is the ability to see the creative source behind
the phenomenal universe. Paul writes: "Now we have
received not the spirit of the world, but the Spirit which
is from God, that we might understand the gifts be-
stowed on us by God. And we impart this in words not
taught by human wisdom but taught by the Spirit . . ."
(1 Cor. 2:12–13). Charles Fillmore writes: "The power
to see in Spirit is peculiar to faith. In its outer expression this power is sight; interiorly it is that which per-
ceives the reality of the substance of Spirit."[13]

Faith is the ability to "see in Spirit." Faith is the
ability to see the underlying reality beyond the appearances of our visible world. Jesus said to his disciples:
"Do you not say, 'There are yet four months, then
comes the harvest'? I tell you, lift up your eyes, and see
how the fields are already white for harvest" (Jn. 4:35).
To "lift up our eyes" is to see reality beyond the appearance. It is the ability to look at the acorn and see
the oak tree within it. This is the power of faith as
Jesus taught and used it.

Jesus taught much about the power of faith. He made
very bold statements about this power. He said to his
disciples, "If you have faith as a grain of mustard seed,
you will say to this mountain, 'Move from here to there,'

and it will move; and nothing will be impossible to you" (Mt. 17:20).

What does it mean to have "faith as a grain of mustard seed"? Some interpret this simile to mean "a tiny bit of faith," but I believe it means much more than that. A seed is a very interesting phenomenon of nature. It is very small but very powerful. The seed contains within it the potential for life—an unlimited amount of life. An apple seed can create an apple tree, which can create apples, which contain seeds, which can create more trees, more apples, more seeds, and so forth. Not just one apple tree lies within the seed. Each seed contains an *infinite* number of apple trees.

The seed is a symbol for unlimited creative power. This is what faith is—an unlimited creative power. Faith has no limit, just as there is no limit to the number of apples that we can produce from one apple seed.

The Reality that underlies all appearances is the reality that underlies your body as well. This Reality is perfect wholeness. This Reality is manifest in the body through the power of faith. Often Jesus would perform a healing with the words "Your faith has made you well" (Mt. 9:22) and "According to your faith be it done to you" (Mt. 9:29). Jesus never claimed to heal by his power alone. He simply had the power to stimulate the faith of others, and it was their own faith that made them whole.

Why Isn't It Working?

We have said much about the unlimited power of faith and yet, we've all had times when we've asked, "Why isn't it working for me?" A variation of this question is: "It worked before—why isn't it working now?" Healing often seems enigmatic. Sometimes we work hard with no apparent results, and sometimes we have miraculous results with almost no effort. Why? I don't know why. But we will explore some possible reasons.

Why isn't it working? One answer is that "maybe it is, but not as quickly as we want." Very often, healing doesn't manifest itself on demand. It may take a steady, persistent effort. This was the case with Myrtle and Charles Fillmore. Myrtle's full recovery took nearly two years of persistent effort. The healing of Charles' withered leg was a slow process of healing taking place over several decades. In our human impatience we may forget that everything progresses according to its own schedule. The human body requires nine months to form itself. The soul also needs time to form and give birth to its new expressions. Jesus tells us, "The earth produces of itself, first the blade, then the ear, then the full grain in the ear" (Mk. 4:28). Life is a process. Healing is often a gradual process.

Another response to "Why isn't it working?" is that "maybe it is, but in a way other than we expect." When we seek healing, we usually have a specific result in mind. The result we seek is usually "a return to normal." We want our bodies or our relationships or our lives to return to what they were or to some idealized image of what they "should be." The forthcoming healing may be a deeper or broader healing than we anticipated. Death may be a healing. Divorce may be a healing. A healing of the soul may not include a healing of the body. The healing may or may not manifest itself according to our expectations. Sometimes the healing is much bigger than we anticipate. All desire for healing is fulfilled when we turn to God for help.

Another question to ask yourself is "Am I holding any doubt in my consciousness?" In the Gospel of Mark is a story of a child suffering from convulsions for many years. The father asked Jesus, "If you can do anything, have pity on us and help us." Jesus replied: "If you can! All things are possible to him who believes." (Again we hear Jesus saying, "It is not my faith that heals, but yours.") The father responded, "I believe; help my unbelief!" (Mk. 9:22–24) As we have seen from an earlier story, this can be a very powerful statement. We may hold "pockets of unbelief" in the subconscious despite our conscious efforts to believe. We may be secretly resisting that which we consciously desire. We need to release these pockets of resistance. It is usually necessary to become conscious of how we are resisting, but not always. If we pray with the willingness to discover whatever we need to learn, then eventually all resistance will be revealed and released.

Another factor that may retard healing is the "hidden payoff." We may be experiencing some "secret benefit" by remaining in a state of suffering or disease. In the Gospel of John is the story of a man who was ill for thirty-eight years. For a long time he lay beside a certain pool of water. The belief was that this pool had healing powers whenever an angel would periodically descend to Earth and stir the waters. The man complained that whenever the angel stirred the water, he could find no one to help him. And whenever he tried to enter the pool, someone always got there before him. Jesus asked him a very interesting question: "Do you want to be healed?" It seems that he wanted very much to be healed, for he lay there for a long time waiting for healing to occur. But Jesus may have seen a hidden payoff and asked the poignant question "Do you [really] want to be healed?" What was the hidden payoff? It's hard to say for sure, but possibly the man had grown accustomed to being a victim and perhaps received alms, and also sympathy, for his plight. If he were healed, it would change his entire way of living. He might have to go to work; he might have to be responsible for himself. "Do you really want to be healed?" Apparently he did, for Jesus said: "Rise, take up your pallet, and walk. And at once the man was healed" (Jn. 5:2-9).

In that same manner that we pray, "Help my unbelief," we may need to pray, "Help me see any hidden payoff in my condition." This will require some courage and honesty, because it's seldom easy to admit to our secret ploys. Yet it will open the door to our healing. "I am willing to be changed" is a powerful statement if we truly mean it.

Rev. Wayne Muller tells of Barbara, a seasoned meditator, who discovered that she had breast cancer. She "confesses":

> I was ashamed to notice on several occasions how I looked forward to telling people that I had cancer, as if that would trick out of them their hidden love for me, their feelings of guilt for having ignored or jilted me. At times the prospect of becoming seriously ill, or even possibly of dying—just to get a break from my own constriction—felt exhilarating. There had been an excitement about all the attention and expressions of love I was getting from friends and relatives at the time of the surgery. I would catch myself imagining my memorial service, people meditating, reading aloud from my journals.[14]

It often takes considerable self-awareness and courage to see and acknowledge these hidden payoffs, but when we do, we open the door for our healing to occur.

When our healing seems not to manifest itself, another consideration is the issue of *release*. Release must precede healing. Sometimes in our quest for healing we become attached to the desired result. The attachment is that of our personal will seeking to "make something happen." Paradoxically, trying to make it happen can keep it from happening. Desire for healing is necessary and conviction in the belief that healing will occur—and indeed is occurring right now—is also necessary. Then we need to let go. If our conviction is complete, then we can rest in the assurance that the work is done. All effort ceases.

An appropriate analogy is that of a farmer who works hard to till the soil, fertilize the soil, and then plant the seeds. Then he lets nature do the rest. With quiet assurance he knows that each seed will produce a plant in a due season. He doesn't dig up the seeds to see if they are growing. He may provide water and remove weeds, but he leaves the seeds alone to do their work.

Just as a grain of seed needs to mature and take root in the soil, so too our seeds of faith need to mature and take root in our consciousness. Letting go may be difficult when a serious challenge threatens us, but it is essential that we do so. We need to do our work and then let God do the rest. This reminds me of a Zen proverb that says: "I sit here quietly . . . doing nothing . . . and spring arrives . . . and the grass grows."

Healing is a mystery. We need to work hard and we need to let go. In the words of T. S. Eliot, we need "to care and not to care."[15] God is in charge, but we must do our part. Through the exercise of faith, we are cocreators in the healing process. We dance with God. Sometimes we lead; sometimes we follow.

Mile Markers

- Faith, like wholeness itself, is a divine idea. It has infinite possibilities for expressing itself. We can truly know faith only through direct experience.

- Faith can be expressed as a so-called miracle, and faith can be expressed in the quiet workings of nature. Its true character is a mystery.

- Faith is the power that makes real the images which are held in mind. According to our faith, our world becomes real to us.

- Reality has an inner and an outer dimension. The body and mind are not separate but are the visible and invisible forms of a deeper reality.

- We begin with conscious desire, yet the deep experience of faith seems to come only after we surrender. Faith is not something we get as much as it is something we allow to enter.

- Quantum physics has reversed the basic premise of Newtonian science, which is that reality is outside of us. Some physicists say that we create our reality with our beliefs.

- Faith is the ability to see the creative source behind appearances—to see the underlying reality. This reality is perfect wholeness.

- Healing may not seem to manifest itself for several reasons.

Chapter Six Notes

1. Elizabeth Sand Turner, *Be Ye Transformed* (Unity Village, Missouri: Unity Books, 1996), p. 168.
2. Michael Talbot, *The Holographic Universe* (New York: HarperPerennial, 1992), p. 90.
3. Ibid., pp. 93–4.
4. Phyllis McIntosh, "Faith Is Powerful Medicine," *Remedy,* November/December 1997, in *Reader's Digest,* October 1999, p. 155.
5. Ibid., p. 152.
6. Deepak Chopra, M.D., *Quantum Healing* (New York: Bantam, 1990), p. 15.
7. Gautama Buddha, "Dhammapada," translated by Thomas Byrom, *Teachings of the Buddha,* edited by Jack Kornfield with Gil Fronsdal (Boston: Shambhala, 1996), p. 4.
8. Fred Alan Wolf, *Taking the Quantum Leap* (San Francisco: Harper & Row, 1981), pp. 127–8.
9. Marilyn Ferguson, "Karl Pribram's Changing Reality," *The Holographic Paradigm and Other Paradoxes,* edited by Ken Wilber (Boston: New Science Library, 1982), p. 21.
10. Ibid., p. 22.
11. Ibid., p. 22.
12. Charles Fillmore, *Prosperity* (Unity Village, Missouri: Unity Books, 1998), p. 43.
13. Charles Fillmore, *Christian Healing* (Unity Village, Missouri: Unity School of Christianity, 1979), p. 89.

14. Wayne Muller, *How, Then, Shall We Live?* (New York: Bantam Books, 1997), p. 196.

15. T. S. Eliot, *The Complete Poems and Plays 1909–1950* (New York: Harcourt, Brace and Company, 1952), p. 61.

Adventure Six

Faith:
The Mind of Wholeness

It is when faith is exercised deep in spiritual
consciousness that it finds its right place,
and under divine law, without variation
or disappointment, it brings results that
are seemingly miraculous.

—Charles Fillmore[1]

In her book *Lessons in Truth,* Dr. H. Emilie Cady[2] talks about two types of faith. She called one type *blind faith,* and she termed the other *understanding faith.* Blind faith is a faith in a power seen to be outside ourselves. It is hoping and trusting that God will do something for us. Understanding faith, on the other hand, is a faith based upon a deep inner knowing. It arises from a personal experience of Truth.

When I was a young boy, I took swimming lessons at the local YMCA. When it came time for me to jump

---

[1] Charles Fillmore, *Christian Healing* (Unity Village, Missouri: Unity School of Christianity, 1979), p. 87.

[2] H. Emilie Cady, *Lessons in Truth* (Unity Village, Missouri: Unity Books, 1999), p. 74.

into the deep end of the pool, I found myself paralyzed with fear. I had seen several others jump into the deep end, so my rational mind knew that I would not drown. Yet my body was not convinced. My mind knew that I would not sink to the bottom but my body hadn't caught up with that knowledge. My first leap into the deep end was based on blind faith. I jumped in trusting the experience of others. I survived. Before long, my leaps were no longer premised on blind faith; I *knew* that I could swim in deep water.

Our evolution of faith is very similar. In spite of many teachings—and perhaps many examples—of the power of faith, we may quake with fear when confronted with a serious challenge. Eventually, we find courage to "take the leap." When we trust, even with blind faith, it builds the foundation for a deeper, more understanding faith. Perhaps we can see that faith exists on a spectrum, where the two types of faith are opposite poles. Perhaps we "move" along this spectrum in a series of miniature "quantum leaps" as we continue to (eventually) choose faith over fear in our life experiences. Inch by inch, crisis by crisis, we move into a deeper experience of understanding faith.

Soul-Talk

I open my mind to the unlimited power of faith.

Write this declaration three times, pausing between each line to allow the statement to saturate your consciousness. Then say it aloud or silently as often as possible each day.

1. _____

2. _____

3. _____

Soul-Thoughts

After you have completed writing your Soul-Talk, take time to sit quietly and observe your thoughts and feelings. Write them down.

1. Make a (brief) list of the times when you have experienced the power of faith in your life. Briefly describe each experience.

2. Referring to the above, do you see any patterns in the way faith has worked for you? Were there any key elements or common factors in the experiences? If so, what does this mean to you?

3. List the times when it seemed that faith did not work for you. Briefly describe each experience.

4. Referring to Activity 3, what patterns or common factors do you see? What does this mean to you?

5. Describe a current situation in your life in which your faith is being called forth. How do you feel about this?

6. Referring to Activities 1–4, what elements do you see present in this current situation? What elements do you see missing?

7. What can you do in your life to develop and deepen your faith? Are you willing to do this?

Off the Main Trail

 Interview a friend using questions 1–4 above. Compare the results with your own experiences.

Stepping-Stone

Keep a "faith journal." Periodically record experiences in which you find your faith being called forth. How did you meet these experiences? How can you use the results of the above exercises to help you in these present experiences? Record your progress and results.

I open my mind to the unlimited power of faith.

Chapter Seven

Love:
The Heart of Wholeness

> All love is divine in its origin, but in
> passing through the prism of man's mind
> it is apparently broken into many colors.
> Yet, like the ray of white light, it ever
> remains pure. It is within man's province
> to make its manifestation in his life just
> as pure as its origin.
>
> —Charles Fillmore[1]

Love is the heart of wholeness. In an earlier chapter we saw that wholeness implies balance, integration, self-actualization. Love is the power that integrates, balances, and actualizes the soul. Hatred wounds and separates us. Love heals and unites. Loving oneself and others is an essential part of becoming whole. And love is the natural expression of wholeness itself.

Love and Healing

Love and healing are interwoven. Genuine love heals all human relationships. To heal a broken relationship is to replace hostility and mistrust with love and trust. Love brings wholeness to our relationships.

Love is essential for healing our psychological wounds.

Dr. Carl Rogers, who developed person-centered therapy, recognized that the three most important factors in a therapeutic (healing) relationship are authenticity, empathy, and an "unconditional positive regard" (unconditional love) for the client.[2] Most psychotherapists and counselors believe that self-acceptance and self-love are important therapeutic goals. Self-love is both the pathway and the product of becoming whole.

The relationship between love and physical healing may not be quite as obvious. Yet love is a key element in physical healing and in the maintenance of physical health. Many physicians have seen evidence of the positive effect of love in healing the body.

Dr. Bernie Siegel tells of a young woman named Evy McDonald who had a severe case of ALS (Lou Gehrig's disease). Her neurologist told her that she had six to twelve months to live. In a letter to Dr. Siegel she wrote: "Death seemed inevitable, and a part of me was truly looking forward to ending this life. Yet I had unfinished business: a strong compulsion to discover what unconditional love was about *before I died*."[3]

In a separately written article, she describes her experiences after she made the commitment to discover unconditional love. She began by sitting in front of her mirror:

> I looked with disgust at my deteriorating body. . . .
>
> I sat in a wheelchair with acutely atrophying muscles. My arms and legs were shrinking. . . .

As I sat in my wheelchair, six months from death, a single, passionate desire pressed to the front of my mind. In my last months of life I wanted to experience unconditional love. . . .

But how could I even hope to realize that goal if I couldn't accept my own body? . . .

The first step was to notice and write down how many negative thoughts I had about my body in the course of each day, and how many positive ones. When I saw the huge preponderance of negative thoughts on the paper, I was forced to confront the degree of hatred I had for my body. . . .

To counter this habitual and ingrained negativity, every day I singled out one aspect of my physical body that was acceptable to me, no matter how small. Next, I'd use that item to begin the rewriting. Every negative thought would be followed by a positive statement . . . . Each day a different positive item would be added. . . .

I couldn't pinpoint just when the shift occurred, but one day I noticed that I had no negative thoughts about my body . . . I was totally at peace, with a complete, unalterable acceptance of the way my body was—a bowl of jello in a wheelchair. . . .

I accepted my body. It didn't need to be any different; it could be whatever it was and whatever it was to be . . . .

My illness was a challenge and a gift. I was stimulated to examine my deepest thoughts, desires and beliefs. The journey of self-discovery restructured my life and led me into a powerful experience of the mind-body connection.[4]

In her letter to Dr. Siegel, she said that her physical body "stopped deteriorating . . . and began reversing the havoc wreaked by ALS . . . . Physical healing did not occur because I set out to 'cure' myself, but because my job on earth [to discover unconditional love] was not complete . . . . Since then, I joyously awake each day, filled with enthusiasm, and continue to play my role in the transformation of medical practice."[5]

Evy's intention was not to change her body but to change her mind. Replacing self-hatred with self-love was a healing in itself. Although this was her primary intention, she received a bonus—a body that began to heal as well. Her intention was not to change her body but to love her body as it was. This was the first and the primary healing. If that were the only healing, it would have been significant in itself. But then her body began to reflect her state of mind, just as it had during the illness.

Evy discovered that the body responds to our attitude toward it. Science is beginning to discover this as well. In recent years, researchers have studied the physiological impact of the experience of love. Research shows that love positively impacts our body. In an article written for *New Thought* magazine, David McArthur summarizes some results of research by scientists working with the Institute of HeartMath:

- When we love, the electromagnetic energy generated by the heart . . . changes from a state of chaos into an ordered, harmonic pattern of waves. This ordered pattern, like a radio wave, affects every cell in the body.

- When we love, the autonomic nervous system that runs the unconscious functions of the body changes from a state of conflict and imbalance into an ordered, efficient, balanced state. . . .

- When we love, the rhythms of the heart change by speeding up and slowing down in a very balanced, healthy and efficient manner reducing stress on the heart and balancing the entire body.

- When we love, many systems in our bodies that were operating independently of each other begin to function together in a state of order and harmony called entrainment. . . .

- When we love, the neuro cortex of the brain, where our higher reasoning functions are stored, is stimulated, bringing us the experience of increased mental clarity and more effective reasoning and decision making power.

- When we love, the stress response in our bodies is reversed within seconds.[6]

Jesus, the Fillmores, and others have taught that love is the greatest healer. It is the healer and the harmonizer of the body, of the mind, and of relationships. Yet its true nature remains a mystery.

The Infinite Expressions of Love

We haven't defined *love*. Perhaps we can't. Love, like wholeness itself, is a divine idea. As a divine idea, love cannot be wholly defined; its essence cannot be captured with words. Love can be experienced; indeed, this is the only way love can truly be known. The experience of love far transcends any description of love.

In her autobiography Helen Keller tells how as a deaf and blind child she learned from Anne Sullivan the meaning of love:

> I remember the morning that I first asked the meaning of the word, "love." This was before I knew many words. I had found a few early violets in the garden and brought them to my teacher. She tried to kiss me; but at

that time I did not like to have anyone kiss me except my mother. Miss Sullivan put her arm gently round me and spelled into my hand, "I love Helen."

"What is love?" I asked.

She drew me closer to her and said, "It is here," pointing to my heart. . . . Her words puzzled me very much because I did not then understand anything unless I touched it.

I smelled the violets in her hand and asked, half in words, half in signs, a question which meant, "Is love the sweetness of flowers?"

"No," said my teacher.

Again I thought. The warm sun was shining on us.

"Is this not love?" I asked, pointing in the direction from which the heat came. . . .

A day or two afterward . . . the sun had been under a cloud all day, and there had been brief showers, but suddenly the sun broke forth in all its southern splendor. Again I asked my teacher, "Is this not love?"

"Love is something like the clouds that were in the sky before the sun came out," she replied. Then in simpler words than these, which at that time I could not have understood, she explained: "You cannot touch the clouds, you know, but you feel the rain and know how glad the flowers and the thirsty earth are to have it after a hot day.

You cannot touch love either, but you feel
the sweetness that it pours into everything.
Without love you would not be happy or
want to play."

The beautiful truth burst upon my mind—
I felt that these were invisible lines stretched
between my spirit and the spirits of others.[7]

When love is experienced, it immediately seeks expression. As a divine idea, love can be expressed in an
infinite variety of ways. There is no limit to the form
of love's expression.

Although we cannot fully define *love* with words, we
can use words to describe certain aspects of love. Charles
Fillmore describes love as "the pure essence of Being
that binds together the whole human family." He goes
on to say, "In Divine Mind, love is the power that joins
and binds in divine harmony the universe and everything in it."[8] Fillmore and others describe love as an
attractive force operating not only in humans, but also
throughout nature—all the way to the molecular and
atomic levels.

Charles Fillmore identified love as one of twelve
spiritual faculties within every human being. Love is
a divine idea operating in various degrees of expression through each of us.

The Jesuit priest and renowned paleontologist Pierre
Teilhard de Chardin said that energy in the universe
has two components: *tangential* and *radial*. Tangential

energy is the attraction of exterior to exterior. This is the energy that attracts atom to atom and molecule to molecule. Radial energy is the attraction of interior to interior. It is the energy that draws elements toward ever greater complexity and ever greater consciousness. It impels all beings to become more than they presently are.[9] This energy is the driving force behind evolution. Teilhard says that radial energy is love. He defines love as *cosmic energy* and describes it as

> The affinity of being with being. . . . The forces of love drive the fragments of the universe to seek each other so that the world may come into being. . . . Love is the fundamental impulse of life. . . . Love alone can unite living beings so as to complete and fulfill them . . . for it alone joins them by what is deepest in themselves.[10]

Both Fillmore and Teilhard say many things about love that are relevant to our exploration of wholeness. Both of them describe love as a divine energy that attracts and harmonizes everything in the universe. Contrary to popular thought, love does not come from us—it comes through us. Love is a divine energy. It is ever-present and eternal. It transcends the individual, yet it operates through the individual. Love is the energy that attracts and harmonizes all elements of creation.

Teilhard says that love is the energy which brings the world into being and causes it to evolve into greater complexity and higher consciousness. This is a very interesting statement about the nature of love. Teilhard saw love as a powerful creative force that is the very foundation of the universe itself—the universe as it is, and the universe as it is destined to be.

Teilhard says that love alone can complete and fulfill us, for it alone joins us together by what is deepest within ourselves. Love is necessary for us to become whole and complete. This reveals a very important point that we will explore in the next chapter. Only by joining together in that which is deepest within ourselves can we become complete and fulfilled. We cannot become whole in isolation from the world around us. Only by knowing that we *are* the world can we experience true fulfillment.

When asked for "the great commandment in the law," Jesus replied, "You shall love the Lord your God with all your heart, and with all your soul, and with all your mind. This is the great and first commandment. And a second is like it, You shall love your neighbor as yourself" (Mt. 22:36-39). This teaching is underscored in the Gospel of John, where Jesus says, "This is my commandment, that you love one another as I have loved you" (Jn. 15:12). Jesus emphasized the power of love in his teachings and he proved it with his life.

Virtually every great spiritual teacher has taught that love is an essential part of becoming whole. Gautama Buddha tells us: "As a mother watches over her child, willing to risk her own life to protect her only child, so with a boundless heart should one cherish all living beings, suffusing the whole world with unobstructed loving-kindness."[11]

Why is love so important? The foundation principle of all Unity teaching is that there is only one Presence and one Power in the universe: God, the Good. Since there is only one Presence and one Power, all beings are expressions of It and are of the same essence. This principle of our essential oneness is a fundamental Truth principle. Love is both the recognition and the natural expression of this fundamental principle. If we are essentially one, then love is the only reality, for anything less than love would be based on a belief in separation from that oneness.

Love requires more than a simple belief in the principle of oneness. Love means living our lives based upon this principle. Although we usually experience love through our feeling nature, it is much more than a feeling. We may experience love through our feelings, but it is expressed in our thoughts, our words, and our actions.

Sometimes what we experience as love is simply a desire to fill our own needs. An attraction for another person can be called love, but it may be an attempt to fill an inner emptiness within oneself. Romantic love and sexual desire, of themselves, are not expressions of love in its fullest meaning. These attractions may eventually lead us to experience love in its true sense. The resulting love, if it is genuine, will far transcend the initial heartthrob. Sometimes romantic love is necessary for us to bond emotionally so that the deeper work of real love can begin.

Genuine love may be expressed within familial relationships—and we hope that it is. Yet what we call familial love may not always be love in the truest sense. As a parent, child, or sibling, our feelings of love may become mixed up with our own need fulfillments or with a sense of obligation. Familial love, romantic love, and sexual desire are important human experiences but these energies alone do not constitute love in its fullest sense.

Love is not always experienced as an emotion. One may engage in a lifetime of selfless service to others without any apparent sentimentality or emotional involvement. Sentimentality or emotional involvement may sometimes hinder the highest expression of love. A minister, counselor, social worker, or health care professional may have a deep love for the people he or she serves without having a strong emotional attachment. A necessary quality for those of us in the helping professions is to be able to experience deep empathy and caring for others and yet not be attached to particular outcomes.

Love as Choice

Author Scott Peck says that love is a choice. He says: "Love is an act of will—namely, both an intention and an action. . . . We choose to love."[12] We cannot always choose feelings of love but we can always choose to act from love. Even if we have strong emotions of fear or anger, we can choose to relate to them with wisdom and love, rather than act them out destructively.

Speaking and acting from love does not necessarily mean suppressing or hiding our feelings. If it is appropriate, we can share our feelings with another without attacking or condemning the other person. We do this by recognizing that no matter what another person does or doesn't do, our feelings are *our* feelings. Our feelings are always our own. If it is appropriate, we may ask another to change his or her behavior or we may set boundaries on the acceptability of certain behaviors. When we choose to love, we can then deal appropriately with another's behavior without criticizing or condemning the other person.

It is from this recognition of love as choice that we can then love our enemies. Indeed, we can love all beings. We can choose to speak and to act from love—no matter what. To experience loving feelings toward everyone may not always be possible. And it is not always necessary. If we can feel loving—great! Yet our words and, especially, our actions form the true expression of love.

Love can be seen as a choice—a conscious act of will. Nevertheless, when we experience full awareness of our oneness with God, love is *not* experienced as a choice. From that consciousness of oneness, love flows as naturally as our breath. Love is experienced as who and what we are; it is no longer a choice that we need to make. From this consciousness we cannot *not* be loving—in thought, feeling, word, or deed. But for those of us who don't live in this consciousness twenty-four hours a day, love can be seen as a choice that we make—moment by moment.

Love is both the path to wholeness and the natural expression of wholeness itself. When we experience wholeness, we open ourselves to the fullest expression of our essential nature, which is divine. Yet in our journey to wholeness, we need to practice love. We need to work at it.

I am not saying that we *should* choose love. If we choose love out of moral obligation or to assuage our guilt, then it's not really a choice. And it's not really love. We are not bad if we choose not to love. The issue here is not about what is good or bad, right or wrong. The issue is about what we choose and the consequences of what we choose.

To love has consequences and not to love has consequences. The consequences are not a reward or punishment from God. They are simply the fulfillment of universal law: "As you sow, so shall you reap." To choose love is to sow seeds that will bear the fruit of wholeness.

All that we have said about love certainly applies to loving oneself as well as another. We can choose to love ourselves at any time. Even if feelings of guilt and self-condemnation arise, we can choose to see them as conditioned beliefs and feelings originating from the past, rather than believe these feelings to be the truth. All feelings of low self-esteem and unworthiness originate from messages given to us long ago. We can continue to believe these "old tapes," or we can choose not to and to love ourselves just as we are. Choosing to love ourselves unconditionally, in this moment, always leads to greater wholeness.

Although we cannot adequately define *love,* we can study some of the expressions of love. The particular expressions that we will discuss are love as *empathy and compassion,* love as *unconditional acceptance,* and love as *forgiveness.* We will look at these expressions of love and their relationships to wholeness.

Love as Empathy and Compassion

Compassion begins with empathy. Empathy is the ability to deeply understand another person's experience. It is not just an intellectual understanding but also a heartfelt, intuitive understanding. Empathy allows us to momentarily see through the eyes of another person. It connects us deeply, person to person, soul to soul. Empathy allows us to experience the other person as a unique and beautiful individual, as precious to us as we are to ourselves.

Empathy is the ability to put ourselves in the other person's shoes, and yet it is also the ability to remove those shoes when it's appropriate. To have empathy is to share another's burden but not to carry that burden for him or her. Empathy heals and empowers both the giver and the receiver.

Every virtue has a "near enemy." A near enemy is a vice that often masquerades as a virtue. The near enemy of empathy is pity. Empathy is different from pity; it is not "feeling sorry" for someone. Pity sees the other person (or oneself) as a victim; it sees her as powerless. Pity is projecting our own belief in powerlessness and victimhood onto another person. It gives us a secret air of superiority, for it keeps the other person powerless and at a distance. Empathy connects us. Pity separates. Empathy empowers others. Pity disempowers others and perpetuates the image of a victim.

Empathy connects us with the unique humanness of another. Empathy can lead to compassion. Compassion is the ability to open our hearts to the experience of another person, and ultimately to all living beings. Compassion allows us to experience the divine in another and in ourselves. Compassion connects us with the divine. By opening our hearts to the suffering of another, we connect with the divine presence within ourselves and others. The word *compassion* means to "suffer with." Very often when we encounter suffering, our response is to recoil, to look away, to rationalize. When we pity those who suffer, we distance ourselves from them; we secretly say, "Thank God this isn't happening to me." To have compassion is not to distance ourselves or recoil from suffering, but to be open to it, to embrace it. In so doing, we open our hearts to the other person. We embrace that person in a deep and therapeutic form of love. We see the divinity within him and within ourselves.

The biblical parable of the Good Samaritan (Lk. 10: 29–37) is a wonderful illustration of the quality of compassion. The robbers who beat the traveler had no capacity for compassion or they could not have done what they did. They saw the man, the traveler, not as a person, but as an object to be exploited, which they did. The priest and the Levite saw the man's suffering and distanced themselves from him. They "passed by on the other side." They undoubtedly justified their actions within their own minds.

But the Samaritan had compassion. He cared for the man as he would have cared for himself. He "went to him and bound up his wounds, pouring on oil and wine; then he set him on his own beast [apparently the Samaritan walked the rest of the way] and brought him to an inn, and took care of him" (Lk. 10:34). Then he said that he would pay the man's expenses for as long as it took for the man to heal. This is a clear example of the quality of compassion.

It is interesting that Jesus chose a Samaritan as the hero in this story, for the Jews despised the Samaritans. Perhaps his intention was to heal the prejudice against the Samaritans. Yet, more likely, he chose a Samaritan because he knew that those who have been victims of suffering themselves are most likely to have compassion for others. Our own suffering is an opportunity to cultivate compassion for others.

Suffering is an opportunity to cultivate compassion but it does not automatically lead to compassion. When we cultivate compassion for our own suffering, we cultivate it for others as well. Those who know what it is to "walk through the valley of the shadow of death" (Ps. 23:4) can readily have compassion for the suffering of others. These folks are often most qualified to

help others in similar circumstances. Many believe
that only those who have been wounded can be effective healers.

Compassion, too, has a near enemy. Perhaps the
term *codependency* is the best description of this near
enemy. The usage of this term has changed somewhat
over the past few years. Originally, *codependency* meant
being addicted to being in (an unhealthful) relationship with someone who was an addict and/or substance
abuser. In its popular usage, the term has broadened
to include any condition of habitually giving up one's
own values, power, or sense of self in order to be loved
or accepted by someone else. The codependent will
vicariously live another person's experiences in an attempt to be loved by that person. This is not motivated
solely by compassion. It is motivated by the codependent's avoidance of his own hidden pain.

Compassion is not codependency. It does not arise
from an avoidance of one's own pain. Codependency
arises from a perceived need for love and approval from
outside oneself. Compassion does not arise from any
such deficiency. Codependency arises from one's own
unacknowledged suffering and unhealed wounds. Compassion arises from our willingness to embrace all our
life experiences—both pleasant and unpleasant.

We cultivate compassion for others as we cultivate
compassion for ourselves. We cultivate compassion
for ourselves when we treat ourselves as friends and
consider ourselves with the same kindness that we
desire from others. We cultivate compassion for our-

selves as we begin to acknowledge our own pain rather than deny it or discount it. To truly love others, we must first love ourselves. To develop compassion for others, we must first develop compassion for ourselves.

Love, as a divine idea, has infinite possibilities for expression. Compassion is a quality of love. It can be expressed in infinite ways. Compassion can be expressed as a feeling, such as a deep sense of warmth and caring. Nevertheless, true compassion is more than just a feeling or intention. True compassion is action. True compassion is kindness, service, and commitment to the well-being of others.

Note that in the Good Samaritan parable the Samaritan didn't just feel compassion toward the wounded man and then continue his journey. The Samaritan took action. He did what needed to be done. He was committed to serving the needs of the wounded man as if they were his own. When we experience our sense of oneness with another, then right action springs forth automatically, because we value the life of another as much as we value our own.

Here's a contemporary story that makes this point:

> An eight-year-old [girl] became ill and was diagnosed with a life-threatening blood disease. A search went out for a donor of blood compatible with her own. As she weakened, no donor could be found. Then it was discovered that her six-year-old brother shared her rare blood type. The mother and their minister

and doctor sat down with the boy to ask if he would be willing to donate his blood to save the life of his sister.

Much to their surprise he did not answer right away. He wanted some time to think about it. . . . After a few days he went to his mother and said, "Yes, I'll do it."

The following day the doctor brought both children to his clinic and placed them on cots next to each other. . . . He drew a half pint of blood from the young boy's arm. Then he moved over to his sister's cot and inserted the needle so that her brother could see the effect. In a few minutes color began to pour back into her cheeks.

Then the boy motioned for the doctor to come over. He wanted to ask a question, very quietly.

"Will I start to die right away?" he asked.

When he had been asked to donate his blood to save the life of his sister, his six-year-old mind understood the process literally. That's why he needed a few days to think about it.[13]

The young boy who thought he was giving his life for his sister expressed compassion in an extraordinary way. Yet do we lack compassion if we are not willing to give our lives for another? Not necessarily. To say that compassion is being willing to give whatever is needed does not imply that it is wrong to put limitations on our ability to give. The question is not *whether* we have limits on our giving but *why* we have them. We may limit our giving out of fear, out of greed, out of a sense of lack. Or we may limit our giving because wisdom and compassion for ourselves dictate that we do so.

On every airline flight I've ever taken, a flight attendant has announced: "In the event we lose cabin pressure, oxygen masks will automatically drop from overhead. If you are traveling with a small child, put on your own oxygen mask first, and then assist the child." The implication is, "If you can't breathe, then you won't be able to help anyone else." To give, we must have something to give from. The compassion which makes us willing to die for another must be balanced with the wisdom which tells us when it is—and isn't—appropriate to do so.

When consciously connected to our Source, compassion flows forth without limitation. Like many great saints and martyrs throughout history, we may be very willing to die for another or for a cause. Yet martyrdom is not necessarily a sign of compassion. Nor does the unwillingness to be a martyr necessarily signify a lack of compassion. True compassion is measured by the openness of our hearts and by our willingness to serve in an appropriate way.

Love as Unconditional Acceptance

Genuine love is unconditional. If love is conditional, if it has "strings attached," then it is not genuine love.

In the story of Evy McDonald's healing, we see that she loved her body as it was, not as she wanted it to be. Yes, we often want circumstances to be different—and we usually want people to be different—but love is acceptance of what *is*, rather than what we want. Paradoxically, when we fully accept what is, we usually get what we want. Resistance, judgment, and condemnation crystallize our lives into rigid, inflexible states. Love opens our personal lives to the natural flow of the greater Life, which is dynamic, ever-changing, and constantly seeking to fulfill our desires.

It's not wrong to want people or circumstances to be different. The problem arises when we make our love or our happiness contingent upon their being different. If the desire for someone to be different arises, then just notice the desire without predicating your love or acceptance of the other person on your desire being fulfilled.

To love others is to accept them as they are, unconditionally. It means to love them if they change and to love them if they don't change. This, of course, also applies to self-love, which is often more conditional than our love for others. Self-love is accepting ourselves as we are now and accepting ourselves as we grow and change in our journey through life. If we truly love a three-year-old child, we will love her just as much at age four and at age five and beyond. Accepting others or ourselves as is doesn't mean that we don't accept change. Yet our love is not contingent upon that change occurring or not occurring.

Unconditional acceptance means accepting not only our friends but also those we might view as adversaries. This brings us to the issue of loving one's enemies. Of all Jesus' teachings on love, this is perhaps the most challenging. "You have heard that it was said, 'You shall love your neighbor and hate your enemy.' But I say to you, Love your enemies and pray for those who persecute you" (Mt. 5:43–44).

Here Jesus is challenging the ancient tribal law of loving our friends and hating our enemies. This antiquated law is practiced with great vigor to this very day. This tribal law was developed to help ensure the survival of a particular nation, tribe, or clan. "It's us against them" is the battle cry uttered countless times down through the ages. Jesus' teaching seems to challenge our most basic human instinct: self-preservation.

To love our enemy, we need to look at what we mean by the term *enemy*. An enemy is someone who threatens us in some way. This threat may be physical, but it usually isn't. The people we dislike the most are generally the ones who threaten our self-images or our belief systems.[14] If someone threatens our physical survival, we can normally take action to protect ourselves. When our self-images are threatened, this seems to be more difficult.

We identify our sense of self with a particular set of mental images and related feelings. This is the self-image. It is who we think we are. The collection of these images and feelings is often called the ego. It may also be called the personality or the false self.

Whatever we call it, it is not who we really are, but it is who we think we are. It is the mind's image of "me." Because of our identification with this image, we feel threatened if that image is threatened. We may feel as threatened as if our physical survival were at stake. Thus we protect this self-image with all the fervor used to protect our lives themselves.

The problem is not with the protective mechanism, for it is biologically programmed into our body-mind system and has ensured the survival of our species for millions of years. If the body is threatened, it may be appropriate to flee or fight. The problem is that this survival mechanism is also used to protect the ego rather than just the body. We have identified with the ego as much as—or more than—we have with the body, so this biological survival mechanism "kicks in" whenever the ego is threatened.

How do we love those who threaten us (that is, the enemy)? If the threat is physical, then we should act accordingly to protect ourselves. If the threat isn't physical, then we really have nothing to protect. We don't need to look at the other person. We need to look at ourselves. We must ask the question "What is it that feels threatened?" Our false selves will be convinced that the "problem" is with the actions or words of someone else. Nevertheless, the real problem lies with our false sense of self. (Once again, it may be appropriate to request that someone change his or her behavior. The real issue, however, is always within us.)

The false self is based on the belief in separation. It feels separate from all other beings. It is this sense of separateness that underlies the feeling of being threatened. The feeling of being threatened, which is fear, creates the sense of an "enemy." We are conditioned to see the external world as real and to believe that the "enemy out there" is real.

If we can turn our attention around and see that the "enemy" is our illusion about who we are, then we have taken a huge step toward loving our enemy. This is a huge step because we have finally located the source of the enemy—within our own minds. By changing our minds we can destroy our enemy, because only in our minds does the enemy really exist.

Remember that love is not necessarily a pink, fuzzy feeling—it is not an emotion. We don't have to like someone to love him. Love is a matter of how we act and how we relate to others. Can we treat everyone with genuine kindness, courtesy, and respect—whether we like that person or not? If so, then we are beginning to love our enemy.

Love as Forgiveness

Forgiveness is virtually synonymous with healing. It is essential to wholeness. Forgiveness can be the most difficult and challenging of all spiritual practices, and yet it may be the most liberating and empowering. Author Sue Sikking writes: "The greatest prescription for a healthy body and a full life is to forgive and forget, to cleanse our own mind that the divine plan of God may be set free to carry on its perfect work of renewal and re-creation."[15]

Forgiveness is cleansing our minds so that the divine idea of wholeness can express itself unimpeded in our minds, bodies, and lives.

Forgiveness is very powerful and yet it is often very challenging. If we look at the condition of unforgiveness— resentment, hatred, guilt—we see that the common denominator is a sense of injustice, a sense that "somebody is wrong." "This shouldn't have happened" or "They had no right to do this" are common thoughts upholding the feeling of unforgiveness. And because of what they did (or didn't) do, we may believe they are bad and deserve to be punished. (With guilt, similar thoughts occur, except they are directed toward oneself.)

Our sense of justice and fairness is very deeply rooted in our individual psyches and our collective psyche. A sense of justice and fairness lies behind the laws that govern our land. When someone or something violates our sense of justice, it challenges our view of how the world should be. From a human perspective, this sense of rightness is necessary. From our viewpoint, certain people do things that are clearly wrong (e.g., rape, murder, child abuse) and violate our basic sense of human decency. We must have laws that protect people from such victimization.

Nevertheless, to forgive, we need to see that our sense of justice and fairness is a human sense of justice and fairness. Our human sense of reality is based upon our senses and our intellect. As humans we operate from appearances. To forgive, we need to surrender our belief in the ultimate reality of appearances and our own sense of justice to a higher reality. This higher reality is not a big judge in the sky but is an exquisite law of cause and effect that operates beyond our human comprehension. To forgive, we must let go of our personal views of justice and embrace a greater vision of justice and order.

Another reason forgiveness is difficult is that unforgiveness seems to protect us from our own pain; forgiveness requires facing this pain. By focusing on another person and on the past, we may attempt to hide from some pain that we are feeling in this present moment. If we feel unforgiveness, it is because we believe that someone has hurt us. Perhaps someone did. If we have been hurt, then healing the wound is necessary. As physical wounds must heal, so too emotional wounds must heal. A big part of that healing lies in facing and discharging the hurt, anger, and grief that are symptoms of being wounded. We must be willing to feel our own pain in order to do this.

To forgive, we must be willing to surrender our own sense of rightness in favor of a higher (and unknown) form of justice. To forgive, we must be willing to face our own pain rather than continue to focus on the perceived faults of another. To forgive, we must be willing to let go. Forgiveness is letting go of all hope for a better past!

To forgive is to let go and let God. The etymology of

the word *forgive* is "to give over, to give away." We forgive when we give our personal beliefs and feelings over to the divine presence within.

Ultimately, forgiveness is a choice: "I choose to forgive." Saying that once may be enough, but usually we need to say it over and over again. Forgiveness can occur in seconds or it can take years but it always boils down to a choice. "Am I willing to let go?" "Am I willing to let go of my personal sense of justice, and trust in infinite Wisdom?" "Am I willing to let go of blaming another and face my own pain?" When the wounds are deep, the process may seem endless. If so, don't worry about it. Be kind to yourself. Just keep looking at the choices in each moment: to blame or to forgive.

If you have intense feelings over something that seems trivial, don't judge yourself for it. Everything reminds us of something else. What looks like a molehill may be the tip of a buried mountain range! Once, a friend borrowed a small amount of money and did not pay me back. I felt hurt and angry. My feelings were way out of proportion to the money involved. As I explored this issue, I could see that I felt disregarded. Exploring this feeling opened the door to a whole flood of childhood memories. All were connected to the experience of feeling disregarded. I could see that all the pain from these experiences was based on the premise that my self-worth depended upon the actions of others. (For children, this is a normal belief but still a false one.) In the process of forgiving my friend for a small debt, I encountered a huge cache of unresolved feelings. And I discovered a deep-seated belief that had been limiting me for a long time.

Forgiveness is difficult work yet it is exceedingly powerful. Forgiveness is a most important activity. We see no greater investment of time and energy than that of forgiveness. Forgiveness is a very powerful expression of love. It connects us with our innate wholeness and, ultimately, with our innate divinity.

Forgiveness and Physical Health

The experience of forgiveness is a very powerful force for healing the physical body. We recall these words of Myrtle Fillmore from Chapter One:

> I went to all the life centers in my body and spoke words of Truth to them—words of strength and power. I asked their forgiveness for the foolish, ignorant course that I had pursued in the past, when I had condemned them and called them weak, inefficient, and diseased. I did not become discouraged at their being slow to wake up, but kept right on, both silently and aloud, declaring the words of Truth, until the organs responded.

Science is beginning to verify what Myrtle demonstrated over a century ago. Research has shown that forgiveness has a positive impact on our physical health. Dr. Sid Sarinopoulos at the University of Wisconsin

published a doctoral dissertation on the relationship
of forgiveness and physical health. Based upon analysis
of data collected, he found the following:

- The more frequently an individual reported
  forgiving an interpersonal hurt, the fewer
  number of different physical symptoms he
  or she reported, both recently (within the
  past two weeks) and over a long period of
  time (examples of symptoms reported:
  headache, sore throat, heartburn, fever, skin
  rash, ear infection, back pain).

- The individuals who reported higher levels
  of forgiveness also reported a lower fre-
  quency of occurrence of a given physical
  symptom.

- Individuals reporting higher levels of forgiveness reported fewer medically diagnosed chronic conditions (examples of conditions reported: diabetes, asthma, ulcers,
  chronic bronchitis, colitis).

- Middle-aged participants who reported
  more instances of forgiveness reported
  fewer medically diagnosed heart problems;
  conversely, those who reported fewer instances of forgiveness, reported more heart
  problems.[16]

Forgiveness is crucial for health reasons alone. Yet if we did research on the effect of forgiveness on prosperity, success in relationships, success in work, and general happiness, I believe we would find an equal (or greater) correlation between forgiveness and well-being. What a wonderful impact it would have on the world if individuals, families, and nations were to practice forgiveness regularly!

If we fully knew the power of forgiveness, we would spend more time in forgiveness than we spend acquiring material goods. Forgiveness is essential to spiritual growth and transformation. Small wonder that among Jesus' last words were "Father, forgive them; for they know not what they do" (Lk. 23:34). He knew that no matter how unjust and horrific the circumstances surrounding his death, he had to be free of all unforgiveness to experience the resurrection. When we see the awesome power of love, we can see why Jesus left us with the commandment: "Love one another as I have loved you" (Jn. 15:12). The power of love to foster wholeness cannot be overestimated. Let us keep working on love—for ourselves and for others.

Mile Markers

- Love is the healer and harmonizer of the body, mind, and relationships. Loving ourselves and others is an essential part of becoming whole.

- Love is a divine idea. We cannot define it. We cannot capture its essence with words. We can know it only through experience.

- Love can be seen as a choice. It begins with an intention. Maybe we cannot always have loving feelings, but we can always choose to act from love.

- Some expressions of love are love as empathy and compassion, love as unconditional acceptance, and love as forgiveness.

- Empathy is the ability to deeply understand another person's experience. It is a heartfelt, intuitive understanding. Empathy is different from pity.

- Compassion allows us to experience the divine by opening our hearts to another's suffering. Compassion is not codependency.

- To love others is to accept them as they are, unconditionally. It means to love them whether they change or they don't change. This also applies to loving ourselves.

- To love our enemy, we need to see that the real "enemy" is our own false sense of self.

We have then found the source of the enemy—it is within our own minds.

- Forgiveness is essential to wholeness. It can be the most difficult and challenging of all spiritual practices and also can be the most liberating and empowering.

- To forgive, we need to surrender our human sense of justice to a higher reality and be willing to face our own pain rather than focus on the perceived faults of others.

Chapter Seven Notes

1. Charles Fillmore, *Keep a True Lent* (Unity Village, Missouri: Unity Books, 1997), p. 31.
2. Gerald Corey, *Theory and Practice of Counseling and Psychotherapy* (Monterey, California: Brooks/ Cole, 1986), p. 107.
3. Evy McDonald as quoted in Bernie S. Siegel, M.D., *Peace, Love & Healing* (New York: Harper & Row, 1989), p. 30.
4. Ibid, pp. 31–2.
5. Ibid., p. 32.
6. David M. McArthur, J.D., "When We Love," *New Thought,* Spring 1997, International New Thought Alliance.
7. Helen Keller, *The Story of My Life* as quoted in *The Treasure Chest,* edited by Charles L. Wallis (New York: Harper & Row, 1965), p. 167.
8. Charles Fillmore, *The Revealing Word* (Unity Village, Missouri: Unity Books, 1994), pp. 124–5.
9. Teilhard de Chardin, *Survival: A Study Guide Based on Teilhard de Chardin's Masterwork "The Phenomenon of Man"* (Pasadena, California: Phenomenon of Man Project, 1972), p. 19.
10. Ibid, pp. 71–3.
11. Gautama Buddha, "Metta Sutta," translated by Thomas Byrom, *Teachings of the Buddha,* edited by Jack Kornfield with Gil Fronsdal (Boston: Shambhala, 1996), p. 5.

12. M. Scott Peck, *The Road Less Traveled* (New York: Simon and Schuster, 1978), p. 83.

13. Jack Kornfield and Christina Feldman, editors, *Soul Food* (New York: HarperSanFrancisco, 1996), p. 11.

14. Our self-images and our belief systems are very closely related. Our belief systems, in the broadest sense, include our image of self and the world around us. They include our sense of what we and the world are and what we and the world should be.

15. Sue Sikking, *Beyond a Miracle* (Unity Village, Missouri: Unity School of Christianity, 1973), p. 45.

16. Sid Sarinopoulos, Ph.D., "Forgiveness and Physical Health: A Doctoral Dissertation Summary," *The World of Forgiveness,* Vol. 3, No. 2, January/February 2000, pp. 16–8.

Adventure Seven

Love:
The Heart of Wholeness

True love must be shared; it cannot
be hoarded. To be blessed by love,
it must be expressed, not repressed.
—Harold Sherman[1]

At the end of this life, when you look back at the road you've traveled, what will have mattered the most to you? What questions will you ask of yourself? I've pondered these questions often, and each time I arrived at the same conclusion. What would matter most to me would have little to do with material success or with intellectual accomplishments. The money I earned and the degrees I acquired would do me little good as I breathed my final breaths.

The questions I would ask are: "Have I loved well? Did I take every opportunity that I could to be kind, to show compassion, to help another? Did I miss any opportunities to forgive, to see beyond the imperfections of another, and to embrace the perfection of his or her

---

[1] Harold Sherman, *How to Use The Power of Prayer* (Unity Village, Missouri: Unity Books, 1986), p. 14.

divinity? Have I loved others as much as I wanted them to love me? Did I love myself as much as I wanted others to love me?" I am happy to be considering these questions now, while I still have time to influence the answers.

When we contemplate the finitude of life, we can see how precious each moment of life really is. This moment is the most precious of all, and in this moment we can choose to love. We can choose to become clear channels of the divine light of love that is our true nature, or we can choose not to. To choose not to love isn't bad. It's just a missed opportunity. Let us not miss any more opportunities.

Soul-Talk

I am a pure channel for divine love.
Write this declaration three times, pausing between each line to allow the statement to saturate your consciousness. Then say it aloud or silently as often as possible each day.

1. _____

2. _____

3. _____

Soul-Thoughts

After you have completed writing your Soul-Talk, take time to sit quietly and observe your thoughts and feelings. Write them down.

1. In a journal, describe yourself as if you were describing another person. What do you like and dislike about yourself? What are the judgments (positive and negative) that you have about yourself?

2. In a journal, list all of the pieces of unforgiveness that you have toward yourself (no matter how minor). Start with the present time and go backward as far as you can remember.

3. Do the same with other people who are in your life. Start with the present time and go backward as far as you can remember.

4. Spend ten minutes (or more) each day forgiving at least one item from each list. State the forgiveness affirmation verbally and then record it in writing. If it feels as though you have succeeded, then cross that item off the list. If not, then leave it on. If you have to "reinstate" some items, then go right ahead and keep working at it. (Be patient with yourself. Don't worry about how long the list is or how long it takes to remove an item.)

5. Write down the name of someone you love. Write down a different name each day. Spend five minutes praying for that person.

6. Meditate on divine love. You may want to begin by chanting the word *love*. After each meditation period, write any insights in your journal.

Off the Main Trail

Who is your "enemy"? Who threatens you? Be honest with yourself. Once you have identified the person or persons, then develop a strategy for loving this person unconditionally. Keep a journal of your progress.

Stepping-Stone

 Today and every day do one act of kindness (no matter how small) for (1) another person, (2) yourself, (3) an animal, a plant, or Earth.

I am a pure channel for divine love.

Chapter Eight

Wholeness and Relationships: You Are Never Alone

> More than any other need, perhaps even
> more than food and shelter, we human
> beings, born of other human beings,
> nurtured by and connected to them,
> need to touch one another. We need to
> stay in contact and acknowledge our
> interdependence and love in order to live
> in a sacred way.
>
> —Jack Kornfield[1]

The quest for wholeness is paradoxical. On one hand, wholeness requires individuation. This requires that we identify and live from our uniqueness, our individuality. The process of individuation usually requires solitude, introspection, going deep into oneself. Yet the quest for wholeness also requires the experience of intimate relationships with others and with all things. We cannot become whole in isolation. We need others and we need the world that we live in.

Who we are extends beyond our physical boundaries. In our quest for wholeness we cannot journey alone because we do not live in isolation. We can neither become whole nor remain whole in isolation from others. We need others as we journey. The divine idea of wholeness includes wholeness in all our relationships. Truly, our journey is not our journey alone.

The quest for wholeness involves relationships because we are intimately related to everything in this universe, whether we recognize it or not. Wholeness itself involves experiencing our intimate connection with all beings. Deepak Chopra tells us:

> We have a very intimate relationship with each other. We have a very intimate relationship with the rest of nature. We have a very intimate relationship with the universe and the more we tune into that intimate relationship, the more likely it is for us to have the memory of wholeness. And once we have that memory of wholeness, it is a lot more than just physical healing because it brings about the spiritual knowledge of our essential state—who we really are. In order to find out who we really are, we have to bond with the universe.[2]

We are spiritual beings having human experiences. Our essential nature is Spirit. As spiritual beings, we cannot experience separation. We can never be separated from anything, for we are one with all. Yet as human beings, we typically experience a sense of separation.

We Are the World

We are one in Spirit but it seems that as human beings we are very separate. This is not so. We are not as separate as we might think. As human beings, we are very much interdependent. We are much more intimate with one another than we might realize.

From birth to death we are dependent upon others. From the time the first humans walked on this planet, the family, the tribe, and the community have been necessary to sustain human life. Today our community includes virtually everyone on Earth; this is certainly evident in the arena of economics and commerce. As I have my breakfast of fruit, cereal, and coffee, I consider the people from many countries who are part of my morning's breakfast: the farmers in the United States who grew the grain, the workers on the coffee plantations in South America and the banana plantations in Central America, the dockworkers, the railroaders, the truckers, the distributors, the grocers, and many others are all part of my morning breakfast. As I go to my closet to get dressed, I find shirts and trousers made in twenty-four different countries. My watch, my computer, and my automobile were all made in other countries. The food we eat, the clothing we wear, the cars we drive, and the gadgets we operate are produced from virtually everywhere on Earth.

We are finding—slowly and painfully—that our fates as humans are tied to the fates of virtually every other species on this planet. They are tied as well to the delicate balance of the ecosystems by which our lives are sustained. The destruction of a forest thousands of miles from where we live can affect the very air we breathe. The pollution from cars and factories on the other side of the planet can impact our local weather for long periods.

The scientific theory called *Chaos* has described a phenomenon known as the "Butterfly Effect." Scientists derived this theory from computerized meteorological models used to make long-range weather predictions. To explain this theory, let's imagine that we have a hypothetical scientist with all the possible data which impacts the weather (for example, air temperature, barometric pressure, wind velocity) from data points one foot apart covering the entire planet, from ground level to the top of the atmosphere. If such data were available, our scientist still could not make a long-range weather forecast with a high degree of accuracy. The Earth's weather system is so complex and its elements are so interrelated that the undetected act of a butterfly fluttering its wings somewhere in China would set in motion forces that could eventually cause an unexpected thunderstorm in New York City![3]

If a butterfly flapping its wings can contribute to a thunderstorm on the other side of the Earth, how can any of us be unaffected by a child's starving to death in Kenya, a dolphin's drowning in a tuna net in the Pacific Ocean, or a forest's being cut down in Brazil? And, by that same token, how can any of us be unaffected by the prayers and kind thoughts of others? We can't be unaffected. We are intimately connected with every living being on this planet.

Deepak Chopra tells us that we are constantly sharing the atoms of our bodies with one another. Based on calculations derived from radioisotope studies, we know that with every breath you exhale, you disburse one hundred billion trillion atoms that were once part of every organ of your body. From these same studies we know that in the past three weeks one thousand trillion atoms have passed through your body that have been a part of the body of every other living being on this planet. And at the present time, your body contains about one million atoms that were at one time a part of the body of Jesus of Nazareth. Long before the days of radioisotope studies, Walt Whitman proclaimed, "Every atom belonging to me belongs to you as well."[4] (It seems that the poets are always ahead of the scientists!)

It is difficult to imagine more intimacy than sharing the atoms of our bodies! Yet there is. We share the same mind. We are psychically connected—to all humans, to all life, to all things. Decades ago the pioneer psychic researcher J. B. Rhine experimentally suggested the existence of telepathy—the ability of thoughts in one mind to be transmitted to others. Since then countless stories of telepathy have been narrated in books and on TV programs. In one interesting case, the Russian psychologist Dr. K. I. Platonov developed the ability to telepathically put people to sleep and then wake them up at distances exceeding a thousand miles![5]

Just as much has been written about telepathy, much has been written about a similar phenomenon known as distant, or nonlocal, healing (many call this *prayer*). Historically, this phenomenon has received little attention from mainstream medical institutions. But in December 1998 forty scientists from universities and research laboratories around the United States gathered at Harvard University for a conference to examine and evaluate data on this phenomenon of distant healing. Preliminary data presented at this conference suggested that we are on the verge of an explosion of evidence to support the efficacy of distant healing. Over the last forty years, more than 150 formal, controlled studies of distant healing have been published—more than two-thirds of them showing significant effects, with a less than one-in-twenty likelihood of the effect having occurred by chance.[6]

Although these studies do not include an explanation of the phenomenon, they suggest that we are psychically connected with one another. Furthermore, our psychic connection not only transcends space, but it may also transcend time. Biologist Rupert Sheldrake recognized a psychic connection among all members of a species. He hypothesized a "morphogenetic field" in which the learning of one member of a species is mysteriously transmitted to all members of the same species with the passage of time.

Although no generally accepted theory exists for these phenomena, many scientists believe that they work because, in reality, we don't have separate minds. Several theories abound regarding the psychic connection of humankind. Dr. Carl Jung postulated the existence of a collective psyche existing within (and beyond) each person. This collective unconscious is not part of our personal memory but is a collective memory from all who have ever lived. Jung developed this hypothesis from his analysis of many thousands of his patients' dreams.

Unity cofounder Charles Fillmore recognized the existence of a "race consciousness" that psychically impacts each of us. Pierre Teilhard de Chardin hypothesized the existence of a "noosphere," a psychic envelope surrounding the Earth and as real as the biosphere and the hydrosphere. Peter Russell suggests that a "global brain" is developing from our interconnectedness. Perhaps the Internet is one manifestation of this global brain or noosphere.

Physically, mentally, spiritually, we are intimately connected with one another. We are not as separate as we may think. We cannot become whole in isolation because, in reality, isolation does not exist.

Aloneness and Relationship

Yet no matter how interconnected we may be in reality, each of us must deal with the personal experience of aloneness. Existential philosophers tell us that every human being struggles with issues of aloneness and relationship. No matter how much we intellectually know of our oneness, each of us—at one time or another—feels alone. In one sense, we *are* alone. No one knows what it's like to be you but you. No one can choose how to live your life but you. No one can live

for you and no one can die for you. In our personal experiences, we each are alone in this journey.

We may attempt to share our experiences with another through words, but words rarely convey the full
meaning of our inner experiences. We are alone in the
world we live in—our private reality. Be it reality or be
it illusion, it's *our* world and we are the only ones who
inhabit it.

Is this private reality a prison that keeps us isolated
and separate, or is it a private studio where we can
create anything we wish? It can be either. The journey
to wholeness requires that we explore our relationships with ourselves as well as with others.

The journey of wholeness requires a deep exploration
of our personal realities. Until we discover the wonder
of our own being, we cannot effectively share that wonder with anyone else. In the condition of wholeness,
we use our intimate relationships to reflect our own
wondrous beauty rather than attempt to find our beauty
vicariously through the eyes of another. Psychologist
Gerald Corey says:

> We alone must give a sense of meaning to our
> life, and we alone must decide how we will
> live. If we are unable to tolerate ourselves
> when we are alone, then how can we expect
> anyone else to be enriched by our company?
> Before we can have any solid relationship
> with another, we must have a relationship
> with ourselves. We must learn to listen to our-

selves. We have to be able to stand alone before we can truly stand beside another.[7]

Herein lies the paradox. To fully appreciate the richness of our relationships with one another and with the universe, we must delve deeply into our own experiences of aloneness. As we fully enter the solitude of our own being, we eventually discover the universe waiting for us—with open arms. Some call this the "hero's journey."

The Hero's Journey

Joseph Campbell identifies the *hero* as one who is a pioneer in consciousness, one who discovers a new way of living and being. The hero then devotes his or her life to helping others in the community benefit from this discovery. Campbell identified an archetypal journey for the hero, and he saw that this archetypal pattern is present in nearly all initiation rituals common among tribal peoples. The journey consists of *separation* from one's community; an *initiation* process, which is experienced in isolation; and then a *return* to the community as a very different person. The hero returns imbued with the power of an encounter with the transpersonal and ready to use that power for the benefit of all.[8]

Before this journey we live in the world and we are of the world. We live according to the standards, values, and beliefs of the community and family in which we grew up. We have not individuated. We are not yet true individuals but are simply products of our environment. (The philosopher Nietzsche called this the "herd mentality.")

The journey begins with separation. We break from the "herd." Often our own unconscious desires for individuation have thrust this break upon us. This is often painful. The more we resist, the more we suffer. We may experience a divorce, a career failure, or a severe health challenge. Some consciously choose to leave the crowd. In any event, we separate.

In the experience of separation, we may feel very alone but eventually we discover a power within that is beyond any worldly power. "For he who is in you is greater than he who is in the world" (1 Jn. 4:4). This is the experience Campbell names "initiation." Initiation is the experience of an imbuement with power from the transpersonal. We touch a Reality beyond our personal reality. This is largely a solitary process, yet we discover that aloneness and solitude can be a great gift rather than a curse, for the fruits of our journeys are extraordinary indeed.

Imbued with a new power, a power not from the world, we eventually return to the world. Yet we return very different from when we left. We return as people who create their world rather than people who are created by it. We return to the world of community and of relationships, but we experience these in a vastly different way.

Before the initiation we were sustained, and perhaps even defined, by our relationships. Then we were spiritual children; now we are spiritual adults. We reenter the world to be in it but no longer of it. No longer products of our past, we now bring forth something truly new and unique into the community of humans. We return to serve, to heal, and to teach our brothers and sisters.

We see a classic representation of the hero's journey in the traditional legend of the Great Struggle of the Buddha:

> The young prince Gautama Sakyamuni set forth secretly from his father's palace on the princely steed Kanthaka, passed miraculously through the guarded gate [separation], rode through the night . . . . Assuming the garments of a monk, he moved as a beggar through the world, and during these years of apparently aimless wandering acquired and transcended the eight stages of meditation. He retired to a hermitage, bent his powers six more years to the great struggle, carried austerity to the uttermost, and collapsed in seeming death, but presently recovered. Then he returned to the less rigorous life of the ascetic wanderer.
>
> One day he sat beneath a tree . . . and the tree was illuminated with his radiance . . . . This was the signal that the moment of his triumph was at hand. He arose and proceeded along a road which the gods had decked . . . .

He placed himself, with a firm resolve, beneath the Bo Tree, on the Immovable Spot, and straightway was approached by Kama-Mara, the god of love and death.

The dangerous god appeared mounted on an elephant and carrying weapons in his thousand hands. He was surrounded by his army . . . . The protecting deities of the universe took flight, but the Future Buddha remained unmoved beneath the Tree. And the god then assailed him, seeking to break his concentration.

Whirlwind, rocks, thunder and flame, smoking weapons with keen edges, burning coals . . . the Antagonist hurled against the Savior, but the missiles were all transformed into celestial flowers and ointments by the power of Gautama's ten perfections. Mara then deployed his daughters, Desire, Pining, and Lust, surrounded by voluptuous attendants, but the mind of the Great Being was not distracted. The god finally challenged his right to be sitting on the Immovable Spot . . . . But the Future Buddha only moved his hand to touch the ground with his fingertips, and thus bid the goddess Earth bear witness to his right to be sitting where he was. She did so with a hundred, a thousand, a hundred thousand roars, so that the elephant of the Antagonist fell upon its knees in obeisance to the Future Buddha. The army was immediately dispersed, and the gods of all the worlds scattered garlands.

Having won that preliminary victory before sunset, the conqueror acquired in the first watch of the night knowledge of his previous existences, in the second watch the divine eye of omniscient vision, and in the last watch understanding of the chain of causation. He experienced perfect enlightenment at the break of day [initiation].

Then for [forty-nine] days Gautama—now the Buddha, the Enlightened—sat motionless in bliss . . . . Then he doubted whether his message could be communicated, and he thought to retain the wisdom for himself; but the god Brahma descended from the zenith to implore that he should become the teacher of gods and men. The Buddha was thus persuaded to proclaim the path. And he went back into the cities of men where he moved among the citizens of the world [return], bestowing the inestimable boon of the knowledge of the Way.[9]

This account of the Buddha's enlightenment portrays the agony and the ecstasy of the hero's journey. Each of us questing for wholeness is on the hero's journey. The stages of separation, initiation, and return are always present in this journey but the journey itself can take many forms.

The mythological representation of the Buddha's awakening may sound somewhat enchanting, and even glamorous, but the real journey seldom is. The real hero may not be a monk sitting beneath a tree in India, but a single mother living in Brooklyn or an African-American male living in South Chicago or a disabled veteran living in Los Angeles. The hero's journey is often invisible to the naked eye; it's hard to see from the outside. Even those on the journey may not recognize it as such—until they reach the end.

Our hero's journey is not necessarily a singular event. We may journey many times during our lifetimes. The separation is not always physical—it may be psychological. We can feel alone in the midst of our own family or community. We may return to our former community or we may return to another.

In returning we see that our journey was not for ourselves alone but was also for countless others whose lives will be impacted by our experiences of wholeness. In returning we see that we are not, and cannot be, separated from any other human being or any other form of life. Our kinship with life extends beyond the human family to include all living beings and, indeed, the entire universe.

The quest is a paradox—the more we individuate and discover our wholeness, the more we realize that we cannot become whole in isolation from others and from our world. The more we each discover our wholeness, the more we realize that what I call "me" extends far beyond the personal self.

For Mahayana Buddhists, the ideal is the *boddhisattva*: "one whose essence is perfected wisdom."[10] Like Gautama, she is a being who, having brought herself to the brink of nirvana, voluntarily renounces her prize that she may return to the world to help others attain enlightenment. The vow of the *boddhisattva* includes the commitment not to desert this world "until the grass itself be enlightened."[11]

Pema Chödrön, a popular Tibetan Buddhist teacher, says:

> Spiritual awakening is frequently described as a journey to the top of a mountain. We leave our attachments and our worldliness behind and slowly make our way to the top. At the peak we have transcended all pain. The only problem with this metaphor is that we leave all the others behind—our drunken brother, our schizophrenic sister, our tormented animals and friends. Their suffering continues, unrelieved by our personal escape.
>
> In the process of discovering bodhichitta [the heart of compassion], the journey goes down, not up. It's as if the mountain pointed toward the center of the earth instead of reaching into the sky. Instead of transcending the suffering of all creatures, we move toward

the turbulence and doubt. We jump into it.
We slide into it. We tiptoe into it. We move toward it however we can. We explore the reality and unpredictability of insecurity and
pain, and we try not to push it away. If it takes
years, if it takes lifetimes, we let it be as it is.
At our own pace, without speed or aggression, we move down and down and down.
With us move millions of others, our companions in awakening from fear. At the bottom we discover water, the healing water of
bodhichitta. Right down there in the thick of
things, we discover the love that will not die.[12]

The return phase of the journey brings us back into
the world in a new way—as new people. Yet we are not
complete upon reentry. Our journey to wholeness includes our bringing the Truth of our inner being into
the world. Only then is it complete. Ralph Waldo Emerson writes: "It is easy in the world to live after the
world's opinion; it is easy in solitude to live after our
own; but the great man is he who in the midst of the
crowd keeps with perfect sweetness the independence
of solitude."[13]

We look at our quests for wholeness in this context.
We see that living in relationship to others is a part of
our journeys to wholeness. We see ourselves bringing
wholeness to our relationships, and our relationships
having the potential to bring us to wholeness as well.

The teacher and student are interwoven. We live in a symbiotic universe where all things are interdependent and are nurtured by their relationships with all other things.

Wholeness cannot exist if we are divided within ourselves or among ourselves. Jesus said, "The kingdom of God is within you" (Lk. 17:21 KJV). The word *within*, in Greek, can also mean "in the midst of you." The kingdom of God is not isolated within us but is within *and* among us. To find the kingdom of God, we must not only look within us but also look *among* us.

Mahatma Gandhi said:

> I want to find God, and because I want to find God, I have to find God along with other people. I don't believe I can find God alone. If I did, I would be running to the Himalayas to find God in some cave there. But since I believe that nobody can find God alone, I have to work with people. I have to take them with me. Alone I can't come to Him.[14]

Gandhi's words speak to a personal experience that I recall. In the mid-1970s I was feeling very stuck in my spiritual progress. When I prayed for guidance, I received an image of an apple tree so heavily laden with fruit that it was about to collapse. This tree needed to share its fruit with others or else it might not survive. I knew that "tree" was me! I had been involved in a long

and intense period of learning; now I needed to share
what had ripened. This image eventually led to my application for the Unity ministerial program.

The Healing Relationship

When Gautama Buddha returned from his initiation experiences, he began to teach others. Many who
have experienced a spiritual awakening and have at-
tained a certain degree of wholeness have a desire to
serve others, often by teaching or healing. Some may
become members of the helping professions or prac-
titioners of the healing arts. Others may do their work
in a less formal way. Either way, the commitment is to
serve.

In whatever form it takes, their service is intended to
awaken others to a higher degree of awareness and to
bring them to a greater degree of wholeness. The work is
not just to fix or even to heal, but to transform. Psychologist Jacquelyn Small calls these people "transformers."[15]

The greatest asset of the effective transformer is her
consciousness. Who we are is more important than
what we say or do. As transformers, we work from the
premise that we are spiritual beings having human
experiences. The answer to every question, the fulfillment of every need, and the healing of every suffering
lie within us as our true nature—which is spiritual.
And, in one sense, the discovery of our true nature is
itself the fulfillment. Our deepest need is not simply to
fulfill our human needs but to discover who and what
we really are.

An effective transformer knows that as spiritual beings, we are always whole and perfect and could never be otherwise. At the same time, she has empathy and compassion for the human condition of suffering. As noted in the previous chapter, empathy and compassion are different from sympathy and pity. We open our hearts to the plight of another but we do not see him as a helpless victim. We see the perfection that he is and yet we know the suffering that he feels. This is called *double vision.*

Double vision is the ability to simultaneously know the suffering of the human being and the perfection of the spiritual being. Double vision is the ability to see someone dying of cancer as a perfect spiritual being without denying in any way the anguish of the human being who lies before us. The mind is confounded by the thought of holding two contradictory ideas simultaneously. The heart has the capacity to hold what the mind cannot fathom.

The Therapeutic Relationship

As we saw in our last chapter, Carl Rogers gave us a formula for functioning as an effective transformer. He said that in any therapeutic relationship the essential elements are authenticity, empathy, and unconditional acceptance of the other person. He formulated this primarily for the psychotherapeutic relationship, but its effectiveness extends to any relationship intended to cultivate wholeness.

Authenticity means being willing to show up as a

human being struggling with human imperfections rather than appearing as a perfect finished product. Authenticity means not hiding our thoughts or feelings but being willing to honestly share them in a responsible way. It means that we don't pretend to know something if we don't. It means that we are willing to risk being honest with another human being. Trust develops from honesty. Healing arises from a relationship of trust.

Acceptance means that we unconditionally accept the value and essential goodness of the other person, no matter what he may have said or done. This does not mean that we condone violence or that we don't set limits on inappropriate behavior. It means that we separate the person from the behavior and unconditionally accept the person despite his behavior. We see the essential nature of the person regardless of his behavior. We address the behavior separately, if necessary.

Empathy, as discussed earlier, is the ability to share deeply in another's experience without judgment and without pity. Empathy entails a deep understanding of the other's experience. It requires transcending the vision of "me and them" and momentarily entering the experience of oneness with another.

Our responsibility is to create a relationship of authenticity, acceptance, and empathy as a foundation for our healing work with another. We may need other professional skills and interventions, but we always begin by creating a relationship based on authenticity, acceptance, and empathy. Very often the relationship itself is more important than our words and technical skills.

Wayne Muller tells a story:

> Yesterday I went to visit Simon, who is dying. He is frightened. He regrets dying alone, with no partner to hold him when he awakens in the night, afraid.
>
> As I sat with him, he wept. He is angry and sad about so many things that he cannot seem to feel the blessings. He is used to controlling the things in his life, and now there are things that cannot be controlled. He is losing energy, losing weight, and he cannot make this stop. I spent much of our time speaking with him about how we can feel the rhythm between sadness and joy, to not get caught in the reasons why. Toward the end of the morning, I felt that some healing had happened; he felt lighter. I believed my words had brought him some comfort.
>
> Then, just before I left, he said, "You know, Wayne, I really don't understand most of what you say." He paused. "But I like your company and the sound of your voice." All the time I thought I was being wise and inspirational, it turned out Simon was soothed by my voice and my companionship. For my

part, I rarely believe my companionship is enough, so I feel compelled to say clever and meaningful things. He wasn't interested. My company and my presence were enough.

Clearly we do not always know our real gift. I assumed my hard-won theological and spiritual wisdom would be the balm that would bring Simon comfort. As it happened, he felt cared for not because of my words but rather in spite of them. As often happens, I went away with a potent lesson, another reminder that I need not work so hard to sound so wise, because that may not be what really heals, not what others need at all.[16]

Healing Ourselves, Healing the World

As transformers many of us see our work being with individuals. Many others see their work extending beyond the individual to the entire human family and perhaps beyond that to include all species and the Earth itself. We realize that none of us exists in isolation. We are deeply connected to all life on this planet. The words "Think Globally, Act Locally" have appeared on many bumper stickers. These words summarize the philosophy of many transformers. In truth *every* act is a global act, whether we realize it or not, because we do not live in isolation.

Just as we encounter people in need of healing, we

see a world in need of healing as well. We see a world filled with many people—six billion (2000 C.E.) and increasing at the rate of one billion per decade. Most of the increase is taking place in the poorer nations. Demographers estimate that our planet can sustain life for about eight to twelve billion people. At the present growth rate, somewhere between 2020 and 2060 our planet could be taxed beyond its ability to sustain human life.

We see a world filled with hungry people, a world where over one billion people are undernourished, and over 33,000 children die of starvation or malnutrition every day. Over a billion people do not have access to safe drinking water. And in this same world, more than $2 billion are spent every day on military expenditures.

The world's problems are not limited to human beings. Plant and animal species are becoming extinct at the rate of more than one per hour. This rate is rapidly accelerating. Seven out of ten biologists believe the Earth is now in the midst of the fastest mass extinction of living things in the history of the planet. Most biologists believe that during the next thirty years, one-fifth of all species alive today will become extinct. Tropical rain forests are disappearing at an alarming rate: an area the size of 3,600 football fields is destroyed every hour. In 1997 twelve million acres of tropical rainforest (an area nearly the size of England) were destroyed. Every year we are losing twenty-six billion tons of topsoil. At this rate there will be none left in 100 years. The carbon dioxide content of the atmosphere has risen by one-third in the past thirty years, adding to the "greenhouse effect," which is contributing to global warming. The ozone layer in the atmosphere, which protects life from the sun's damaging ultraviolet rays, is rapidly being destroyed by pollutants.

Much healing is needed. Yet God is present in all of it. We need not despair nor should we be complacent. God *is* present, but not as some magical figure in the sky who will swoop down and save us from our greed and ignorance. God is present *as* us. We are God's hands and feet. We are both the cause and the potential cure for the suffering on our planet.

It is time for us to wake up and to grow up. These words of Chief Seattle ring ominously in our ears: "This we know—the earth does not belong to man, man belongs to the earth. All things are connected like the blood which unites one family. Whatever befalls the earth befalls the sons of the earth. Man did not weave the web of life; he is merely a strand in it. Whatever he does to the web, he does to himself."[17]

Personal Wholeness and Planetary Transformation

Personal wholeness and planetary transformation cannot be separated. As a personal transformation is preceded by an initiation process, so too may be a planetary transformation.

Transpersonal psychologist Christopher Bache writes:

> The intensity of suffering that many people engaged in inner work are experiencing now derives from the fact that we are not just doing our own personal work. At a certain level, we are all engaging the transpersonal, the collective consciousness. And not just at the species level—perhaps the whole planet is in some sense going through a very powerful transformative crisis, much as in Paul's letter to the Romans where he said that "the whole creation groaneth and travaileth in pain together."[18]

Once again, we hear that "we are the world." Who we are as individuals cannot be separated from who we are collectively. The work of personal transformation and the work of helping others in the process are essential parts of planetary transformation.

If our planet itself is experiencing an initiation, then our angst may be good news after all. This is the opportunity to create a way of life beyond materialism and rationalism. Perhaps this is our planetary "rite of passage" that will take us into spiritual adulthood where we are no longer children of God but adult partners of the divine. We are ready to become conscious cocreators.

As children we were dependent; as adolescents we tried to be independent; as adults we are learning to be interdependent. Perhaps this current stormy era is a period of humankind's self-centered adolescence. Being adolescents, we may be ready to experience the rite of passage that takes us into planetary adulthood. Maybe we will learn that happiness comes only from a state of wholeness and that that state of wholeness must include all of us.

Perhaps the Nobel Prize-winning physicist Albert Einstein best summed it up with these words:

> A human being is a part of the whole, called by us "Universe," a part limited in time and space. He experiences himself, his thoughts and feelings as something separated from the rest—a kind of optical delusion of his consciousness. This delusion is a kind of prison for us, restricting us to our personal desires and to affection for a few persons nearest to us. Our task must be to free ourselves from this prison by widening our circle of compassion to embrace all living creatures and the whole of nature in its beauty.[19]

We are spiritual beings having human experiences. Our purpose is to create a life of wholeness for each of us and for our brothers and sisters (of all species) who share this planet with us. Our challenge is to become both fully human and fully divine as we journey together in our quest for wholeness.

Mile Markers

- In our quest for wholeness we cannot journey alone because we do not live in isolation.

- The quest includes all our relationships because we are intimately related to everything in this universe. We cannot become whole in isolation from others.

- No matter how interconnected we are in reality, each of us must deal with the personal experience of aloneness.

- Joseph Campbell identifies the hero as one who is a pioneer in consciousness, one who discovers a new way of being. Each of us questing for wholeness is on the hero's journey.

- The quest is a paradox—the more we individuate and discover our wholeness, the more we realize that we cannot become whole in isolation from others and from our world.

- Many who have experienced wholeness desire to serve others, often by teaching or healing. They intend their service to bring others to a greater degree of wholeness.

- The foundation for our work as transformers is to create therapeutic relationships. The essential elements are authenticity, empathy, and unconditional acceptance.

- As transformers our work may be with individuals, the human family, or Earth itself. We are deeply connected to all life on this planet.

- The planet needs much healing. We are the cause and the cure for the suffering in our world. Personal wholeness and planetary transformation cannot be separated.

Chapter Eight Notes

1. Jack Kornfield in Kornfield and Feldman, *Soul Food* (New York: HarperSanFrancisco, 1996), p. 115.
2. Deepak Chopra, "Quantum Healing Workshop" at Unity Temple on the Plaza, Kansas City, Missouri, October 6, 1991.
3. For more information on the "Butterfly Effect" see James Gleick, *Chaos: Making a New Science* (New York: Viking Penguin, 1988), pp. 20–1.
4. Walt Whitman as quoted by Chopra.
5. K. I. Platonov as quoted in Sheila Ostrander and Lynn Schroeder, *Psychic Discoveries Behind the Iron Curtain* (Englewood Cliffs, New Jersey: Prentice-Hall, 1970), p. 97.
6. Elisabeth Targ, "Distant Healing," *Noetic Sciences Review*, August–November 1999, No. 49, p. 24.
7. Gerald Corey, *Theory and Practice of Counseling and Psychotherapy* (Monterey, California: Brooks/ Cole, 1986), p. 80.
8. Joseph Campbell, *The Hero With a Thousand Faces* (Princeton, New Jersey: Princeton University Press, 1973), p. 30.
9. Ibid., pp. 31–4.
10. Huston Smith, *The World's Religions* (New York: HarperSanFrancisco, 1991), p. 124.
11. Ibid.
12. Pema Chödrön, *When Things Fall Apart* (Boston: Shambhala, 1997), p. 91.

13. Ralph Waldo Emerson, "Self-Reliance," *Essays by Ralph Waldo Emerson* (New York: Harper & Row, 1926), p. 38.

14. Mahatma Gandhi as quoted by Nelson Mandela, "The Sacred Warrior," *Time*, December 31, 1999, p. 126.

15. For more information see Jacquelyn Small, *Transformers: The Therapists of the Future* (Marina del Rey, California: DeVorss, 1982).

16. Wayne Muller, *How, Then, Shall We Live?* (New York: Bantam Books, 1997), pp. 245–6.

17. Chief Seattle as quoted in Peter Russell, *Waking Up in Time* (Novato, California: Origin Press, 1998), p. 41.

18. Christopher Bache as quoted in Richard Tarnas, "The Great Initiation," *Noetic Sciences Review*, Winter 1998, No. 47, p. 29.

19. Albert Einstein as quoted in Howard W. Eves, *Mathematical Circles Adieu: A Fourth Collection of Mathematical Stories and Anecdotes* (Boston: Prindle, Weber & Schmidt, 1977), p. 60.

Adventure Eight

Wholeness and Relationships: You Are Never Alone

Heaven is my father and earth my mother
and even such a small creature as I finds
an intimate place in its midst. That which
extends throughout the universe, I regard as
my body and that which directs the universe,
I regard as my nature. All people are my brothers
and sisters, and all things are my companions.
　　　　　　　—Chang Tsai, eleventh century[1]

We usually think of ourselves as individuals, separate entities. This is, of course, true but only in part. The reality of who we are cannot be contained within a layer of skin or described by a biography. The wind which blows across the sky is as much a part of you as the breath which moves through your lungs. We once knew this in our personal infancies; we experienced no separation from our mothers or from the world around us. In humanity's infancy we knew our oneness with Mother Earth and with all nature. As we grew up, in-

[1] Chang Tsai as quoted in Joel Levey and Michelle Levey, *Living in Balance* (Berkeley: Conari Press, 1998), p. 156.

dividually and collectively, we forgot this basic sense of oneness with others and with our world.

Perhaps we are being forced to remember this now that we see the price of separation. We have known our oneness and we have known our separateness. Perhaps it is time to know both simultaneously. Like the electron, which is both particle and wave, we exist as particulars and we exist as oneness. We can know personal wholeness only as we remember our oneness with all life. The more we discover the depths of our own being, the stronger the memory becomes.

Soul-Talk

I am one with all life.

Write this declaration three times, pausing between each line to allow the statement to saturate your consciousness. Then say it aloud or silently as often as possible each day.

1. _____

2. _____

3. _____

Soul-Thoughts

 After you have completed writing your Soul-Talk, take time to sit quietly and observe your thoughts and feelings. Write them down.

 1. Write about the times when you felt a strong sense of connection with your world and/or with life itself. What were you doing? What triggered the experience? What ended it?

2. List the people in your life you feel the most connected with. What is it about your relationships with these people that create this sense of connection?

3. Write about a time when you felt isolated, lonely, or disconnected. How did you handle that experience? What triggered it? What ended it?

4. Write the name of someone who is your teacher, healer, or mentor. What qualities does that person possess which make him or her effective? In what way are you brought into greater wholeness in this relationship?

5. If you were to experience a greater sense of personal wholeness, in what way would the relationships in your life be changed? Give some specific scenarios.

6. What can you do to cause a greater sense of wholeness in the relationships in your life? What would it take for you to do this? How would you go about doing it?

Off the Main Trail

Write about a hero's journey in your life. Identify the separation, initiation, and return phases. How were you brought into greater wholeness because of this journey?

Stepping-Stone

 Each day take some specific action to cause a greater state of wholeness in your relationship with (1) another person, (2) humanity, and (3) nature. Keep a journal of each action and of any impact these actions have on you or others.

I am one with all life.

About the Author

Robert Brumet is chairperson of Pastoral Studies and Skills in Unity School for Religious Studies at Unity Village, Missouri.

Brumet teaches courses in spiritual counseling, transpersonal psychology, and meditation. He also conducts seminars and programs on a wide variety of topics related to spiritual growth. He has presented his programs at churches and retreat centers throughout North America and the Caribbean. He is author of the popular Unity book *Finding Yourself in Transition* and a contributing author to *New Thought for a New Millennium*, also published by Unity. He has authored several articles in *Unity Magazine* as well as many Unity pamphlets. His lectures, seminars, radio broadcasts, books, and magazine articles have impacted the lives of thousands of people.

Robert was ordained a Unity minister in 1980 and has served Unity churches in Evansville, Indiana, and Overland Park, Kansas. Before entering the ministry, he was a director of systems analysis for a Michigan manufacturing firm and an adjunct professor at two colleges in western Michigan. A native of Toledo, Ohio, he received B.S. and M.S. degrees from the University of Toledo.

In his leisure time, Robert enjoys tennis, fly-fishing, bridge, writing, and meditating. He has four grown children and six grandchildren. He resides in Kansas City, Missouri.

In case you missed out on the first two books in the Continuing Quest series . . .

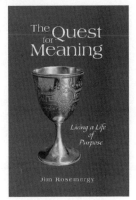

The Quest for Prayer:
Coming Home to Spirit
Mary-Alice and Richard Jafolla

The authors of the original and best-selling *The Quest* and *Adventures on the Quest*, Mary-Alice and Richard Jafolla, will help you discover that the journey of life is a quest for spiritual rediscovery which leads you back to yourself. You will come to an understanding of what prayer is, why we pray, whether prayers are always answered, and much more.

$10.95, softcover, 140 pp., ISBN 0-87159-241-X, **#82**

The Quest for Meaning:
Living a Life of Purpose
Jim Rosemergy

Jim Rosemergy will help you look inside yourself to discover your purpose here on Earth, add meaning to your life, and find fulfillment in everything you do. Learn to dance with the question *Why*.

$9.95, softcover, 134 pp., ISBN 0-87159-222-3, **#11**

To order, call Customer Service at 800-669-0282.

P00638